D0845068

Praise for *Intentional Leadership*

"Having worked closely with Rose M. Patten for close to three decades, through a time when Canadian institutions have been repeatedly acknowledged among the tallest trees in global finance, I have awaited the arrival of this book with great anticipation. Patten has a deep understanding of the power of decision frameworks in problem-solving, in business strategy, and on broad issues. She argues persuasively for the reconciliation of divergent stakeholder interests through rigorous, observation-based thinking while maintaining an empathetic view of human motivation. In a world defined by uncertainty and polarization, she builds a compelling case for intentional leadership and explains eight capabilities for leaders to achieve their full potential, both in early and in accomplished stages of leading."

William Downe, C.M., Former CEO, BMO Financial Group

"Rose M. Patten is an incredible resource on the subject of leadership, with hands-on experience in a multitude of highly successful organizations in the business and the public sectors. As a superb leader herself, a lifetime student in both the art and the science of leadership, and a natural innovator, Patten offers approaches that are progressive and cutting-edge yet thoughtfully grounded. Having viewed her in action from a wide variety of stances, I can't think of a more authoritative source on the subject of leadership and can personally attest that her ideas deliver huge and lasting benefits for individuals and organizations."

Donald Guloien, President, Guloien Capital, and Former President and CEO, Manulife

"Rose M. Patten is a proven senior leader in the banking sector and in academia. Her depth and diversity of experience resonates throughout this book. Patten provides powerful leadership observations and a leadership framework attuned to the complex challenges facing all leaders today. Unlike some books that put forward easy, snappy answers, *Intentional Leadership* looks at the enduring and fundamental pillars of leadership – making it more relevant and meaningful."

Wilma Vreeswijk, Former Deputy Minister/President, Canada School of Public Service

"While there are numerous books on leadership, this work stands out as it is built on a variety of real-life experiences. Leaders across sectors were interviewed, many at the height of the COVID-19 pandemic, resulting in very timely insights on leading through disruption and change. This easy-to-read book makes clear that in this complex and rapidly evolving world, leadership requires an open mind, adaptability, and resilience. Rose M. Patten makes clear that leading today requires a good understanding of oneself, clear personal values, and the ability to collaborate with a diverse set of partners."

Vivek Goel, President and Vice Chancellor, University of Waterloo

"In a world of dramatic change, leaders must change too! This is the key message of Rose M. Patten's *Intentional Leadership*, and one that I wholeheartedly support. At the Center for Creative Leadership, we have long developed leaders who make a difference in their organizations and in the world through the power of creative, human-centered leadership. These qualities are now more important than ever as leaders face a host of complex challenges that require new capabilities. As Patten writes, 'leadership is *not* timeless. What got us to here in the past has changed.' She outlines key shifts in the context of work that require leaders – both experienced and new – to become more intentional about how they lead and to cultivate new mindsets and practices for leading. I have had the pleasure of working with Patten over the years to develop BMO's top leaders. In every instance, she has shown herself to be a passionate expert, advocate, and advisor. In this book, she draws from her lifetime of experience in distinguished business and academic positions to provide a valuable resource and leadership framework enabling leaders to meet the challenges of today and tomorrow."

Mark Holt, Organizational Leadership Practitioner, Center for Creative Leadership

"Why should you read this new book on leadership? First, because traditional business models and management and leadership practices need updating. Rose M. Patten proposes the concept of intentional leadership – with a focus on eight capabilities for leading effectively, grounded in the new workplace reality. Second, because this book is easy to read and grasp. Its structure, with short chapters and a logical flow of learnings, makes it an appealing and digestible read. And third, because the author is credible on the subject. Throughout her successful career – in the vanguard of female Bay Street financial executives, rising to the executive committee of BMO Financial Group in addition to other distinguished leadership positions – Patten has exemplified stellar leadership and personified the qualities and capabilities she advocates for in this book. To be clear, if you are in a position of leadership – in the private, public, or nonprofit sector, or if you have a general interest in the subject – you should read this book."

Anne Golden, Canadian Administrator, and Former President and CEO, the Conference Board of Canada

"The title of this book is so telling. Rose M. Patten has a rich background as a leader in corporations and public institutions. Beyond her direct leadership roles, she has selected and developed leaders, mentored leaders, and built relevant institutional leadership capabilities. It is an impressive record. But what makes Patten uniquely impressive is that she is constantly – intentionally – thinking about what is needed now and as the context changes."

James Fisher, Professor Emeritus, Rotman School of Management

"I have watched Rose M. Patten's responses, in real time, to the changing demands that leaders constantly face. It is clear, for those leaders who embrace change, that Patten's intentional leadership practices are timely, compelling, and straightforward. She makes a powerful case for being an intentional leader and going beyond instinct and yesterday's assumptions. Patten also explains eight critical capabilities – the 'Big 8' – to address pressing challenges in human-centric leading and dynamic strategic environments. This is a must-read for anyone who wants more from their leaders, embraces self-renewal, and strives to increase their own impact. Patten offers practical and tested insights in a range of leadership contexts, gained in her own distinguished and diverse leadership career, and that of other accomplished leaders. At BMO Financial Group, we have adopted and implemented the 'Big 8' capabilities, and we see the importance of practicing intentional leadership."

Mona Malone, Chief HR Officer and Head of People and Culture, BMO Financial Group

INTENTIONAL LEADERSHIP

THE BIG 8 CAPABILITIES SETTING LEADERS APART

Rose M. Patten

ÆVO UTP

Aevo UTP
An imprint of University of Toronto Press
Toronto Buffalo London
utorontopress.com

© Rose M. Patten 2023

All rights reserved. No part of this publication may be reproduced, stored in or
introduced into a retrieval system, or transmitted in any form or by any means
(electronic, mechanical, photocopying, recording, or otherwise) without the prior
written permission of both the copyright owner and the above publisher of this book.

Library and Archives Canada Cataloguing in Publication

Title: Intentional leadership : the Big 8 capabilities setting leaders apart /
   Rose M. Patten.
Names: Patten, Rose M., author.
Description: Includes bibliographical references and index.
Identifiers: Canadiana (print) 20220412006 | Canadiana (ebook) 20220412022 |
   ISBN 9781487508876 (cloth) | ISBN 9781487539184 (EPUB) |
   ISBN 9781487539177 (PDF)
Subjects: LCSH: Leadership. | LCSH: Success.
Classification: LCC HD57.7 .P38 2023 | DDC 658.4/092 – dc23

ISBN 978-1-4875-0887-6 (cloth)   ISBN 978-1-4875-3918-4 (EPUB)
                                   ISBN 978-1-4875-3917-7 (PDF)

Printed in Canada

We wish to acknowledge the land on which the University of Toronto Press
operates. This land is the traditional territory of the Wendat, the Anishnaabeg, the
Haudenosaunee, the Métis, and the Mississaugas of the Credit First Nation.

University of Toronto Press acknowledges the financial support of the
Government of Canada, the Canada Council for the Arts, and the Ontario Arts
Council, an agency of the Government of Ontario, for its publishing activities.

Canada Council
for the Arts

Conseil des Arts
du Canada

ONTARIO ARTS COUNCIL
CONSEIL DES ARTS DE L'ONTARIO

an Ontario government agency
un organisme du gouvernement de l'Ontario

Funded by the   Financé par le
Government   gouvernement
of Canada   du Canada

Canadä

MIX
Paper from
responsible sources
FSC® C016245

Dedicated to Thomas Di Giacomo, my husband, friend, and forever advocate who is with me every step of my journey – in career and in life – his love, care, and humor are limitless.

Contents

PART TWO: LONG-HELD BELIEFS, MYTHS, AND HABITS – CHALLENGES TO LEADERS' SUCCESS

PART THREE: THE BIG 8 CRYSTALLIZES – SETTING LEADERS APART

PART FOUR: LEADERSHIP STARTS WITH YOU – IT MUST BE INTENTIONAL

Preface: How This Book Evolved

A lifelong interest in leadership and a career across multiple sectors and geographies prompted this formal exploration of leadership and what it means. It began in 2012, in the aftermath of the global financial crisis, a time when no sectors were exempt from the disruptions it had brought, the scandals it revealed, the failures that ensued.

Now, a decade later, prompted this time by the unique demands of a lengthy and highly disruptive pandemic, I have been drawn once more to leadership and what it means. Has leadership evolved in response to such challenging and changing circumstances? Will it continue to evolve? What do leaders need to be successful? Can we pinpoint the specific *capabilities of leadership* that will now be even more critical to success and more highly valued and sought?

In exploring such questions, I developed a leadership framework that I call "the Big 8." Since 2014, the Big 8 capabilities have been defined and tested in business schools and executive classrooms. They have been adopted by senior leaders in corporate settings and in the public and not-for-profit sectors in North America and beyond. Today, as we emerge from the aftermath of an even-more unprecedented global upending – this time from the COVID-19 pandemic – we are seeing once again the real-time impacts of the quality of leadership and how much it matters. Leadership is in the spotlight, more transparent than ever, shining bright and exposed.

Leadership: Never More Important – Never Harder

What does this light reveal? That decisions and influence by leaders span so many day-to-day life survival issues for the well-being of citizens – whether it be mental health, erosion in economies, family hardships, job losses, ruined businesses. Leadership does matter, and, correspondingly, attention to leadership is greater. Concerns continue – as they should – over how leaders have responded and whether they have stepped up by renewing their approaches and capabilities. Much is at stake. Continuing to scrutinize and make sense of how leaders can be better is an obligation for all of us.

Reframing It!

The spotlight on leadership has moved to *how* people lead in challenging and changing circumstances. Innovative models, digitalization, technologies – these are all important. But what matters more is how leaders lead other people. We see how this has become increasingly predominant in recent years. CEOs and boards are more actively speaking out about the need for better leadership. Research studies have shown that the quality of leadership is not hitting the mark for today's challenges. The organic ability to grow the next generation of leaders is also troubling. A multiple-year study of over 2,000 emerging leaders in 100 organizations worldwide has found that 90 per cent of "just random moves" of such leaders actually result in failure. In fact, the belief that high performers mean high potential for leadership is now being called into question.

It is against this somewhat discouraging backdrop that I felt it was time to bring forward to a wider academic and public audience the insights emerging from my close-up study of leadership; these have underpinned the importance of the Big 8 capabilities and leading with intention. I am fortunate in this work to have the generous contributions of accomplished and wise leaders who share the passion and defining moments of their own journeys. As this book will reveal, their stories and insights add value and inspiration to everyone who embraces the hope for leading better and making sense of its essence.

Embracing It!

This book is aimed at a broad audience, as all of us are leaders at one time or another in our lives and careers. Good leadership happens when someone, by intention, has a positive impact – whether through empathy, inspiration, or wisdom. While some people seem to do this naturally, *most of us – if we have the will – can learn it and continue to do it better.* The book, as you will see, is not a prescription. Rather, it is the sharing of learning acquired through the experiences and practices of leaders over two-to-three decades. Each chapter is aimed at enabling the reader to discover and make sense of the essence of leading well. We will meet and examine the Big 8 – the indispensable capabilities for leading well. These capabilities are intended to respond to the individual leader and the human side of leading effectively. Everyone can examine the Big 8 for what they mean on an individual and personal basis. Accordingly, everyone will have different capabilities, depending on how they respond to each of the Big 8. It's for you to decide how to cut the cloth and what fits best! But it has to be based on having the will to lead better and lead well.

I hope you will join me on this journey of discovery of *leading better through intentional actions*. Our journey unfolds through twenty-three short, digestible chapters, organized into four parts.

Why Leadership Is Harder

The introduction enables you to reflect on *why* leadership needs increased attention and how "defining moments" can truly impact the paths taken by successful leaders. The evidence presented will show that leadership can be learned and that it can – and does – evolve with meaningful consequences through thoughtful intentions. Stories of their own "defining moments" are generously shared by accomplished leaders from diverse backgrounds. These confirm that "defining moments" emerge in every leader's journey. They can come from small of big personal happenings – or from unprecedented crises, as you will see.

Unmistakable Game Changers

Part 1 answers the question of why leadership is hard. We focus here on the emergence and impact of what I call "unmistakable game changers" – from which no leader is exempt and to which all leaders must respond with renewed capabilities. The unmistakable game changers are each identified and discussed.

Mindset – Beliefs

Part 2 moves from the external to the internal. That is, from the externally driven unmistakable game changers to the individual leader's personal beliefs about leading. The leader's mindset, and the influence of long-held beliefs and myths, are identified and explored. We see the flaws of outdated thinking that can unconsciously impede a leader's success. Part 2 answers the question: What are the contrasts in the skills and abilities that leaders need now, as compared with what was traditionally valued in leaders? Such contrasts, which have very real impacts, are depicted as the swing of the leadership pendulum in another direction. I call this the "pendulum shift." Compelling affirmations emerge clearly showing the shift *from* instinctive leadership *to* intentional leadership and *to* the principle that leadership can be learned, as long as one has the will and intention. The corollary to this is that leadership is *not* timeless; it must be renewed constantly.

Defining Capabilities for Now

Part 3 crystallizes the Big 8 capabilities, which are at the core of a leader's personal leadership. Your tour will stop at each of the eight capabilities. You will hear how each fits within the leader's overall role and co-resides with the other dimensions of essential capabilities – for example, strategic leadership, organizational leadership, business leadership, and so forth. Part 3 provides examples of how the Big 8 are combined and incorporated into a leader's role as complex challenges occur.

Applying It!

Part 4 brings us to the question of "Now what?" At this point of the journey, we are reminded that leadership starts with you, me, us – the leaders. This last part provides the "takeaways" and "how-tos"

Leaders Engaged in Deliberate Conversations for This Book

Marc-André Blanchard is the EVP and Head of CDPQ Global Investment Group and Global Head of Sustainability at CDPQ. This role includes coordinating CDPQ's international operations and overseeing the sustainability orientations, activities, and strategy to integrate ESG factors into all investment activities. Before joining CDPQ, he was Canada's Ambassador and Permanent Representative to the United Nations in New York. Prior to that, he was chair and CEO of McCarthy Tétrault, one of Canada's leading law firms. Present directorships include co-chair of the Investor Leadership Network. He is a member of the UN Global Investor for Sustainable Development Alliance; member of the World Economic Forum's Global Future Council; member of the board of the Montreal Heart Institute Foundation; and chair of the Principal's Global Advisory Council of the Université de Montréal. He has served on several other boards related to health, the United Nations, and NAFTA.

Mary Anne Chambers is chancellor of the University of Guelph. She has been an executive of one of Canada's major banks, a cabinet minister in the Government of Ontario, the governor of a Canadian Crown corporation, and the director of a publicly traded corporation and of several not-for-profit organizations. An Order of Ontario, a Meritorious Service Medal, the Queen Elizabeth II Diamond Jubilee Medal, the Golden Jubilee Medal of Queen Elizabeth the Second, and four honorary doctorates are among the many awards that recognize her contributions to Canada.

Ron Farmer is a managing director at Mosaic Capital Partners, a private investment firm. Before joining Mosaic, he was a senior partner at McKinsey & Company. In his twenty-five-year career with the firm, he held several leadership positions, including sitting on McKinsey's board of directors, co-leading the global e-business practice, and serving as managing partner for the Canadian practice. He is a director emeritus at McKinsey and an honorary director at the Bank of Montreal.

Meric Gertler was appointed president of the University of Toronto in 2013. He is one of the world's foremost authorities on cities, innovation, and economic change. He has advised governments in Canada, the US, and Europe, and such international agencies as the OECD and the EU. Founded in 1827, the University of Toronto is one of the world's leading research-intensive universities. Its global outlook and cosmopolitan location bring together top minds from every conceivable background and discipline to collaborate on the world's most pressing challenges. All while providing more than 97,000 students across three campuses with knowledge and competencies to navigate our rapidly changing world.

Mary Jo Haddad has had an illustrious thirty-year career at Toronto's Hospital for Sick Children, culminating in a celebrated ten years as president and CEO. Mary Jo is a seasoned director holding positions at Telus Corp as chair of the HR and Compensation Committee. She is past director of the TD Bank Group and Vector

Institute; an inaugural board chair for MaRS Innovation (TIAP); and the founding chair of Children First Canada. She is founder and president of MJH Associates. Named to the Order of Canada in 2010 for her leadership in children's health, she has received numerous other awards, including being named as one of Canada's inaugural Top 25 Women of Influence in Health Sciences and receiving the Canada's Most Powerful Women: Top 100 Award.

Tiff Macklem was appointed Governor of the Bank of Canada in 2020 for a seven-year term. As Governor, he is also chair of the board of directors of the Bank and a member of the board of directors of the Bank for International Settlements. He is chair of the Group of Governors and Heads of Supervision, the oversight body of the Basel Committee on Banking Supervision, and co-chair of the Financial Stability Board's Regional Consultative Group for the Americas. Before becoming Governor, Tiff was dean of the Rotman School of Management at the University of Toronto. During the 2008–9 global financial crisis, he was Associate Deputy Minister at the Department of Finance Canada and represented Canada at the G7 and G20 summits and at the Financial Stability Board.

Barry Perry has spent most of his successful career with Fortis Inc. (TSX/NYSE: FTS), serving as president and CEO from 2015 through 2020 and, before that, as executive vice-president and CFO for more than a decade. He led Fortis through a period of transformational growth; Fortis now ranks among the top utilities in North America. He has prepared a strategic push for growth in the United States with a strong focus on sustainability. He currently serves on the boards of CPP Investments and Capital Power Corporation.

Janice Gross Stein is the Belzberg Professor of Conflict Management in the Department of Political Science and the founding director of the Munk School of Global Affairs and Public Policy at the University of Toronto. She is a Fellow of the Royal Society of Canada and an Honorary Foreign Member of the American Academy of Arts and Sciences. She was awarded the Molson Prize by the Canada Council for an outstanding contribution by a social scientist to public debate. Her research focuses on the intersection of geostrategy and public policy. She has received honorary doctorate of laws from universities in Canada and abroad and is a member of the Order of Canada and the Order of Ontario.

Kathleen Taylor has had an impressive multifaceted career holding top leadership responsibilities across multiple sectors, beginning with being the president and CEO of Four Seasons Hotels and Resorts, with world-wide responsibility. She is currently the chair of the board of the Royal Bank of Canada (RBC), Altas Partners LP, and Toronto's Hospital for Sick Children, and serves as a director of Air Canada, CPP Investments, and the Adecco Group. She has received numerous business and leadership honors over the course of her diverse career and is a member of the Order of Canada.

Darryl White was appointed CEO of BMO Financial Group in 2017. Prior to this he was CEO of BMO Capital Markets. BMO Financial Group is the eighth largest bank in North America with assets providing personal and commercial banking, wealth management, and investment services to 12 million customers. He is a member of the Business Council of Canada, the U.S. Business Council, and the Mayor of Beijing's International Business Leaders Advisory Council, and he serves as a director of the Bank Policy Institute (BPI). He is co-chair of the Inclusive Local Economic Opportunity Roundtable, a partnership between BMO and United Way Greater Toronto that develops approaches to increasing economic opportunities in the Greater Toronto Area. He is chair of the Catalyst Canada Advisory Board and serves on the board of Catalyst, Inc.

Acknowledgments

So many people deserve my gratitude for their constant support in the production of this book. I was surrounded by a wonderful, dedicated team who went above and beyond in the editing, the research, the development of graphics, and other related activities.

John Barrett, who was my editor from day one, also supported additional projects along the way. John meticulously summarized the rich stories of the ten senior leaders with their diligent thoughts conveyed thoroughly. He was a valuable sounding board throughout. John's wife, Maurie, was also there along the way as editing took place. I am grateful to both.

Jaime Krause, whose contributions spanned research, design, and production as well as thought partnership across many elements. Jaime's supportive role goes beyond this book and her unique and broad-ranging talent is constant, in judgment, value added and getting things done.

Sheena White, with her creative and artistic skills, enabled us to complete the final graphics to further convey key messages and give valuable visuals to the reader.

Hana Black, my longtime executive assistant, always stepped up for the office-related activities that emerged with producing this book, willing to do whatever was needed.

Brenda Ichikawa, a colleague from another part of my privileged work, listened with keen interest, quietly asked questions, and provoked helpful thoughts.

Karen Collins, such a talented leader and colleague whom I value tremendously. Always there to support and identify other talent such as most of the professional resources mentioned above, and to assist on the journey.

My great thanks to each and all. I am indebted to you for your dedicated and professional support.

Introduction: Putting the Spotlight on Leadership

Defining Moments: Leadership Can Be Learned

An important realization from my years of working closely with many leaders and observing them in action – especially in responding to crisis and new circumstances – is that *leadership can be learned*. Successful leaders invariably have experienced a *defining moment* in their careers from which they have emerged as better leaders. Whether through response to crisis, adaptation to changing context, or self-reflection and awareness, defining moments are both real and consequential for leadership.

Defining moments in one's leading happen when we reflect and go beyond instinct to take *actions with intention*. This is proven not only by a crisis of massive proportions, like the 2007–8 global financial crisis, the current COVID-19 pandemic, or others such as the 9/11 attacks. It can also be seen in many personal turning points. Everyone has turning points. We just need to reflect deliberately on them, study their implications, and take away learnings. Belief about utilizing turning points or disruptions to advantage propelled this study of how leaders can adapt and renew themselves; and how leaders can be more impactful in transforming their strategies, tactics, and connections with others, and be more tuned in to their present circumstances and contexts.

Adaptability – Renewal Emerges

Putting the spotlight on successful leaders reveals a defining moment – a turning point, a change of course, an adaptation to context. But do such things actually happen in real life? Are leaders aware of these moments? Moreover, if they believe they've been successful in leadership to date, are they capable of adapting, even if they realize the circumstances and context demand it? This is where we turn to the actual experience of leaders. We learn about their encounter with defining moments, as well as the need for courage, for adaptability, for renewal in one's leadership.

In preparing this book, I have had the great honor and joy of deliberate conversations with accomplished and admired leaders to hear their stories of challenges and learnings. You will meet them all as they recount their leadership experiences and insights from positions at the top. They include corporate and other sector top leaders, such as CEOs, chairs of boards, ministers of the Crown, an ambassador, a university president, and academics. All have been instrumental in this attempt to locate the essence of leadership. All have willingly joined me in the shared quest to constantly improve and renew the capabilities of the leaders, especially needed for the times we are facing and those we will face in the future.

My conversations with these leaders reinforce how important a defining moment can be. And it's very different in each individual's experience. For example, Mary Jo Haddad tells of a defining moment during the financial crisis meltdown. She had been CEO of a very large hospital for only a couple of years when it happened. As she recounts: "The big challenge was to break the log-jam on space limitations. But in the midst of a crash, how was this to be done? Rather

Seize the moment with boldness.

than withdraw, I prepared for the board with a big plan. Everyone thought I was out of my mind, trying to raise so much money at such a time." Despite this, she succeeded. What Mary Jo learned at that moment both renewed and refined her leadership. For a crisis is also a time to aspire to greater things. As she puts it: "I don't want to focus on what we can't do; I want to know what needs to happen, what needs to be true." I could only marvel at the courage and willingness she showed in thinking differently and acting with such intention.

Mary Jo's story illustrates that a defining moment must be seized. But how? Here, Tiff Macklem's experience in academia and government helps us understand how the context of the moment can define both the challenges that leaders face as well as the capabilities needed to surmount them. Leaders, he says, need *strategic agility* in disruptive times as well as the *intention to lead differently*. "It's depressing to say, but history shows that one bad thing leads to another. So, when something bad happens, leaders must think ahead, imagine what else could go wrong, and start preparing for what's next."

The global financial crisis and, before that, the Great Depression, he says, illustrate the knock-on effect of decisions taken during difficult times. They can inadvertently trigger outcomes not intended or fully anticipated (e.g., the dot-com bubble, 9/11, the 1998 Asian currency crisis). "That's why leaders must think today of what tomorrow's problem will be. You've got to get ahead of crises to stop them. Would anyone have predicted that G7 governments would have effectively suspended capitalism and guaranteed all their large banks in order to restore confidence in the wake of the global financial meltdown in 2008? Unimaginable, but that's what happened. In 2020, would anyone have believed that all the schools would be shut due to COVID-19 – even if you'd told them a week before they were closed? Unimaginable." The context demands something more than problem-solving. Leaders are good at solving problems, Tiff tells us, but that is not enough. "In a crisis there are no surgical solutions. You are past that. Instead, you need to overwhelm and crush the problem. You are going to have to do something you've never done before. Something you never imagined you would even be considering."

Leadership Grows, Never Stops

Katie Taylor has a diverse career in hospitality, health, and banking. She speaks passionately and persuasively about her own leadership journey and leadership learnings. "Leadership is learned by our changing contexts, whether it is a big crisis or other conditions. Learning to lead never stops!" She worries about the tendency of many leaders to react to the moment with a tried-and-true mindset that may not reflect insights or differences in the situation at hand. Nor will a mindset that was proven useful in the past grasp the longer-lasting implications of a current crisis.

Most important, however, is the lost opportunity in crisis situations for leaders to renew their thinking. Such renewal implies personal adaptability, which is now such an imperative for leaders. What, though, drives this imperative? In Katie's view, it is propelled by culture and social environment, in particular an organization's stakeholders and not the shareholders only. Renewal requires agility, letting go of the tried and true. As she puts it: "Ten years after the global financial crisis, we see the companies that really took it to heart by reinvesting their cultural fabric and strategic direction. Others, however, continued doing the same thing as before just as soon as they'd righted the ship and satisfied the regulator. And what happened? Five years later, we get a sales practice issue at Wells Fargo."

A Continuum of Sustainability

Leaders manage their businesses for the long-term and not just to today's advantage. This means recognizing how the social environment is changing while adapting to those changes. As Katie calls it, a "sustainability continuum" and the "multi-stakeholder way of thinking about your business":

> From a cultural fabric perspective, Canada is different than the USA. We think differently. Canadian banks have long had a variety of stakeholders; they couldn't just ignore them and steam ahead. When you look at companies that have gone through crises and how they respond to such events – the key word is sustainability. Does your social license (or credibility) continue to exist? Leaders who have moved their companies along the "sustainability continuum" are respected. The pandemic illustrates this. For example, everyone says employee safety is paramount – and some said it even before the pandemic struck. But the pandemic has actually made companies do things.

Yes, it's true, as Katie and others point out, we have seen many company successes, failures, or setbacks during recent upheavals. Many are attributable, rightly so, to the strategies in their operating models that CEOs now admit were held for too long or were flawed. Hindsight reveals that leaders have not led as well as was needed. Yet we know of other instances where leaders excelled through the many extreme challenges, showing that leaders can indeed adapt and renew their practices in real time, even as disruptions hit. Mastering adaptive learning and personal adaptability have become a require-ment, even table stakes, in today's environment of continuous disrup-tions and change. I am reminded of Peter Drucker's quote: "If you want to learn something new, you have to stop doing something old."

The real-life experiences shared by Mary Jo, Tiff, and Katie convey much about the essence of leadership. Their actions and reactions to defining moments and changing contexts point to their courage, adaptability, continued renewal, and deliberate intention to let go of past practices that might have worked before but now do not. They each illustrate the principle of *leading by intention* and not just by instinct.

Can people expect defining moments in their own leadership jour-neys? Not only is the answer "yes," but it is desirable if you aspire to lead well. Darryl White describes the hazards for leaders who are locked into yesterday's assumptions on which past practices were formed. "One comes to expect a major dislocation in one's professional career these days. That's what's changed from previous environments. And yet lots of young managers can be very rigid on their career paths. They will inevitably experience difficulties, given the volatility and disloca-tions of today and in the future. It's hard to coach them to expect this."

Losing a Fixed Mindset!

In other words, how does one become more adaptable when things already work for you? Do you stay with what brought you this far and helped you achieve many successive and successful feats? And can one be "too old to change"? In answering such questions, each person has to look to themselves – and into themselves. I will do so by offering a glimpse of how I was forced to become more adaptable and intentional early on in my career, and how it became a norm for the rest of my journey.

My strong belief is that leadership is learned, and that defining moments and crisis offer welcome paths to strategic agility and leading well. This belief has arisen from many real-life experiences – not unlike those of Mary Jo, Katie, Tiff, and others. Over my career, I have held diverse roles in the different pillars of banking, each with different cultures, markets, regulatory bodies, and missions. This provided me with a constantly changing universe of stakeholders and shareholders – in Canada, the United States, Europe, and Asia. When a leader, by choice or happenstance, is exposed to broad and diverse cultures, new and different rules, different ways of thinking – there is no doubt of the necessity to question one's own stance, to pause before assuming tried-and-true techniques, and to lead with intention.

My own learnings about leadership sometimes happened the hard way. Here's where Mary Jo's story of courage and determination strikes a chord as I think back on similar situations – being in tough leadership situations where failure is not really an option. I learned reflection and intention from the late John MacNaughton, whose mentoring brought light to my natural habit of "leaving little to chance." But the roots of my reflection can be found in my mother's admonition. "Rose," she would say, "don't just do something, sit there!" Reflecting, learning, adapting – and the fortitude to "stick with it" – these can become life habits. And when they do, leadership moves away from instinct to consultation and actions become *intentional*.

Such experiences led me to think deeply on the capabilities that renew and improve leadership in a world of increasing complexity, crisis, and social expectations. Ron Farmer's words reinforce this approach: "A leader cannot rely on past experiences as in the past. Experience is valuable and enables one to see things, to recognize a playbook of things encountered before or managed before. Those have helped in the past but cannot be relied on with the new reality of today. Too many factors are different and changing real time." He and I and others in this book wholeheartedly share the view that leaders are made, not born. And if they are made, then leadership skills can be learned and developed – and must be renewed constantly.

Don't just do something. Sit there. "Reflect."

Today's focus on leadership will only increase the attention we need to pay to how we choose leaders in the first place. Does context shape leadership or do leaders shape context? This study will show unambiguously that context defines leadership! Which then brings us to the question raised at the beginning of this introduction. What do we need to believe in to be successful leaders and how do we need to think differently about leadership? The next four chapters of part 1 will answer this complex question.

FIGURE 1. What We Need to Believe

PART ONE

Leadership Has Never Been Harder – The Changing Context Drives It

CHAPTER ONE

Today's Unmistakable Game Changers: No One Is Exempt

We have already put the spotlight on leadership and why it needs increased attention. We have heard, through stories of accomplished and enlightened leaders, why leaders need to refresh and renew how they lead. It is because of the ever-changing contexts brought on by continuous disruptions and crisis. In this chapter, we share their personal insights on how leaders can step up to such challenges.

Disruptions – Lasting Game Changers!

As we reflect on these examples, we still need to make sense of what the biggest causes are that compel leaders to change. Of course, it is natural that disruptions often bring about change. But can we identify *dramatic and unmistakable game changers* from which no leader is exempt? Can we look beyond the proximate causes to find what drives the themes and pathways for leadership renewal? In other words, those things that are here to stay and will continue to shape how we need to lead.

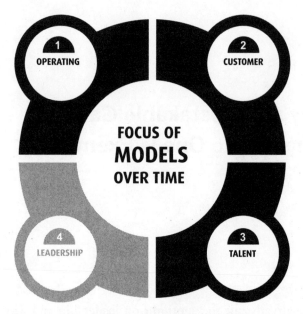

FIGURE 2. New Business Models Have Emerged while Leadership Models Lag

Organizations have indeed responded to the unprecedented speed, interconnectedness, and uncertainty of change. We witness new and innovative business models, new operating models, new customer service approaches. We also see increased attention paid to talent management and leadership models. We see many organizations embracing these contextual disruptions and grappling with the change in mindsets needed to cope with them managerially.

However, we see fewer organizations fully examining the true implications for the senior leaders. And yet they are the ones relied upon to make changes happen in their organizations; they are called upon to inspire their groups, to engage others, to empower employees – and to lead well. It was in making sense of the real impetus for leaders to better understand and be influenced by why change is required that this book, and the work supporting it, got started. I began to explore what was really changing the game for leaders. It increasingly appeared to me that what had gotten leaders to where they were would evidently not keep them there. Nor would it get them to where they needed to go.

What is so different? To find the answer we must address the first question, What is fundamentally so different and confronting leaders in such a prominent way – and in a manner that will only deepen in rigor, expectations, and perpetual demands? And then the second question, What specific capabilities do leaders need more of, in order to lead effectively through these demands and to be better leaders?

As we have found in the introduction, the answer does *not* lie in assuming that the tried-and-true practices used before will hold us in good stead. We must avoid that age-old pitfall. Albert Einstein's well-used quote about not solving significant problems of today with the same level of thinking we had before is poignant here. Comfort with one's past success is a natural human tendency. However, it can blur judgment and leave a false sense of confidence. This blind spot is common; nobody can say they have perfect 360-degree vision. Recognizing this fact helps us determine whether leadership is "timeless" (as we will explore in part 2) and whether leaders who believe this run the risk of becoming complacent.

Yesterday's Assumptions Linger On

Ron Farmer highlights both the potential and danger of complacency on the part of CEOs and leaders more broadly. They now have to be much more tuned in to what's around them while hitting the ground running. In recalling consulting with a big North

American automaker in Detroit at a time when CEOs did not have to take account of competitors to the same degree as they do today, Ron illustrates his point about complacency in leadership. "There was a time when people appointed to leadership positions had a honeymoon period to cruise around the organization and get a read on what they wanted to do. They had a year and a half to look at things, evaluate potentially disruptive impacts, and react accordingly. They don't have that luxury today for sure. Today, organizations, boards, and stakeholders have less and less patience, and leadership must be prepared for and respond to this constant sense of urgency." Ron goes on to question the notion of born leadership, noting that the distinction between intentionality versus instinct in leadership is very valid for the following reason: "Successful leaders must adjust to a quickly changing environment. Little wonder they turn to consultants for strategic advice, because one's experience and 'pattern recognition' may not be relevant to the changing context."

Complacency Is Alive

A story about the trap of complacency was told by the late David Foster Wallace in a speech at Kenyan College in Ohio. "There are these two fish swimming along and they happen to meet an older fish swimming the other way. The older fish nods at them and says: 'Morning boys, how's the water?' The two young fish swim on a bit, then eventually one of them looks at the other and says 'What the hell is water?'" The point is that complacency and comfort zones can make leaders oblivious to the reality around them, especially if it's changing.

Katie Taylor expresses her concern that complacency is still a danger; that even now, after such an unprecedented upending as the COVID-19 pandemic, there is a risk that leaders could fall back to the same methods of leadership as before; that they could do so without enough reflection on, or courage to really change, their habits and beliefs. "Adrenalin is really pretty powerful in one's body. Some people are able to lift cars. But how long does the rush last? When the pandemic hit, we started very strong – leaders everywhere did step up. But through the darkness of winter, fatigue set in and we got tired of things." Her worry and criticism focus on the lack of long-term thinking about the lasting impact of disruptions and on the recourse to more familiar "short-termism." "As big issues are tackled, people tend to flip to quick fixes at the expense of tackling core changes, which is hard to do and always much more difficult than you think."

Forbidding Complacency!

It is therefore important to identify the unmistakable game changers that forbid complacency and the reaching back for previous or short-term approaches and solutions. Getting a handle on these will help us analyze what drives the need for continuous renewal of leaders' mindsets and practices; how they analyze, see around corners, and devise strategies; and how they shape the norms for leading themselves now and others in the future.

What, then, are the unmistakable game changers that took hold in the last decade in a powerful way and changed our organizations in significant ways? My analysis, supported by research and reflection, lands on three such game changers that are head and shoulders above the rest, and that definitely make leadership harder:

1. Increased stakeholder expectations – beyond shareholders
2. The ever-changing workforce and workplace – with its multi-generational and intercultural mix
3. Short-lived strategies and digital dominance

The next three chapters examine each of these unmistakable game changers. Once we understand them better, we will be ready to travel on to the Big 8 capabilities. There we will embark on a journey of self-discovery and intentional leadership. The Big 8 is not a prescribed list of attractive traits nor a prescription to be followed. It is a process of self-reflection and renewal, of finding your way toward intentionality in leadership and placing your human-driven capabilities front and center.

Renewal is for everyone, as Peter Drucker points out: "It is easier to go from great to greater than it is from average to mediocre."

FIGURE 3. The Three Unmistakable Game Changers

CHAPTER TWO

Game Changer #1: Increased Stakeholder Expectations

Over the past decade, the true meaning of stakeholder expectations has been defined and become well established across multiple economic and social sectors. Increased governance across institutions has reflected this: we see adoption of significant policies, codes of conduct, controls, and regulations. We can once again point to the pivotal period following the global financial crisis, as we witnessed with shock the fraud, deceit, and scandals being revealed everywhere.

The impetus for regulatory transformation emerging from that time has permeated many sectors. That crisis laid the groundwork for many of the foundations we see in place today. Perhaps the most transformative regulation began with the implementation of the Sarbanes-Oxley Act in the banking sector. But regulatory changes have not been confined to financial institutions. The impacts of governance and stakeholder changes have been felt in other sectors – including, for example, health, education, government, as well as the media.

Today, we continue to see trust erosion across all sectors. For example, the 2022 Edelman Trust Barometer[1] shows data based on

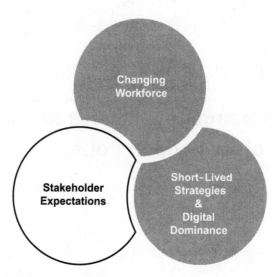

FIGURE 4. Stakeholder Expectations

the general population (unless otherwise noted) highlighting that distrust is now society's default tendency: "Nearly 6 in 10 say that their default tendency is to distrust something until they see evidence that it is trustworthy." When distrust is the default, we then lack the ability to debate or collaborate.

Trust but Verify

It is comforting that most leaders now see these strengthened controls, regulations, and policies as "business as usual" and "as it should be." Trust in our institutions still remains on trial as continued verification is demanded. It reminds me of President Ronald Reagan's quote during the Cold War when rivalry between the United States and the Soviet Union was at its height. His three words that guided the American negotiating position on reaching any agreement with the Soviets were "Trust but verify."

A prominent and wide-ranging change arising from the ruins of crisis is stakeholder expectations. So much so, that I call it one of the three unmistakable game changers. It has deep and lasting implications for leaders and leadership.

Stakeholders – beyond Shareholders

Mary Anne Chambers helps us understand this unmistakable game changer by describing what it has meant for her and how we have to think and lead differently. She believes an indicator can readily be seen in how businesses use the term *stakeholder*. For example, do the bank directors now talk about stakeholders or is *shareholder* still the dominant term?

> Previously, bank directors used to talk about shareholders and stakeholders, often emphasizing only the former. That's all different now. Broader stakeholder interests in every sector are so critical to recognize. Examples abound. Instead of shunning students protesting the relationship of big banks with the university, they are members of the governing council where their voice is heard. When they demonstrate with placards about tuition, you emphasize ways to show them they matter. They are stakeholders – the primary reason why the university exists; they pay tuition and want to feel respected and appreciated.

Mary Anne raises an important fact. In recent years, all stakeholders, including suppliers and society at large, have been given more consideration. Certainly, the pandemic has illuminated this unmistakable game changer for leaders. It provides the leader with the opportunity to correct or enhance their multistakeholder models and, most importantly, it reinforces the need to check one's mindset around the *co-existence* of stakeholders, well beyond the traditional concept of shareholder.

Stakeholders are not some intangible group "out there." They are part and parcel of how an organization survives and thrives. Your customers are stakeholders. But so too is your staff. Without a broad understanding of the co-existence of your stakeholders, it will be impossible to navigate tricky situations, such as that which Mary Anne recounts in an incident with an irate bank customer. The bank staff – backed by senior executives like herself – must look after the abusive customer's interests as a bank stakeholder. Yet, at the same time, she had to look out for her staff, who are also her stakeholders. What did she do? "I connected with the customer and proposed a solution for him to continue to be our bank's customer and to treat staff appropriately. As both were stakeholders, the interests of both had to be protected, especially as staff cannot always easily defend themselves, but a leader can intervene."

Understanding the co-existence of stakeholders from a leadership perspective shows us another aspect of this unmistakable game changer – and that is *character*. Mary Anne says it better than anyone:

> Today, leaders face so many expectations in the area of corporate social responsibility to stakeholders – whether it be a just civil society, inclusion, diversity. This is far above and beyond expectations of the past, which focused mainly on the financial bottom line. The character traits of leaders are also on display. They need to earn respect not as CEOs and senior executives, but as human beings; they gain respect through their actions, not just through seniority. In fact, expectations for leaders may even be higher than ordinary people these days.

Mary Anne's insights speak to the real essence of leaders and the increasing challenges they face, as stakeholder expectations become

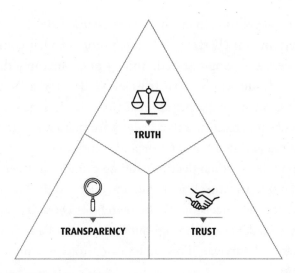

FIGURE 5. The Three Ts of Character

more deeply developed and become the norm everywhere. Greater *transparency*, greater *trust*, and always *truth* are shaping the norm with more personal responsibility and more explicit accountability becoming the table stakes for leaders.

The Three Ts: Trust Is on Trial

This new paradigm for governance and obligations to stakeholders across all sectors can be thought of as the three Ts of "truth, trust, and transparency." It's all about character and a greater *certainty of character*. The implications go well beyond the usual oversight and controls expected by boards and regulators. Increasing stakeholder expectations now result in deep and broad attestations and verifications (and yes, sometimes raising the hackles of CEOs and other leaders). It is steadily settling in and will continue to be a new reality wherever trust and truth are openly and unabashedly questioned.

It is no exaggeration to say that *trust is on trial* in leadership. Which is why certainty of character is a much more explicit consideration when leaders are being assessed. And it's not something that is "one and done": leaders must earn trust every day. Greater moral certainty is expected. The motivations behind leaders' actions are also being questioned to ensure that leaders are in no way self-serving in their choices and decisions. Clear and transparent reasoning is expected to underpin each decision and be evident in discussions and debates. In other words, leaders need to speak to the "why" not just the "what" of their decisions.[2] The search for certainty of character and trust in leaders runs throughout every facet of an organization's well-being and survival. This includes customers, employees, and community.

Customers Insist on Trust

Customers have rising expectations. They continue to increase their expectations explicitly in products and services, but also implicitly for transparent confirmation that a company's reputation, its ethics, and its moral fiber are evident in the decisions they make. They want more than the often-well-stated formal principles or corporate values that they see published. Research over time has shown that over 60 per cent of customers' purchasing behaviors are influenced by evidence of ethical standards and the CEO's character.

This fact may go unnoticed or underappreciated by leaders. Of course, determining whether customers stay or leave based on the character and reputation of the CEO might be subtle and potentially more relevant to some organizations than others. We can understand that it is missed when companies get caught up with the competitive nature of products and services, prices and the like. But it exists. Character matters. Moreover, an organization's stakeholders – that is, its customers, employees, community – seek to verify their trust on a continuing basis. This should be recognized by the organization in each of its strategies.

Character Is King

Barry Perry speaks with conviction on the linkage of leadership character and stakeholder demands. To him it is game changing and increasingly visible, not just a silent assumption. "Today, there are stakeholder demands at all levels – it is not just about regulators, employee demands, community expectations, and of course customers. Leaders must digest it all and set a path for success with those considerations and criteria. It calls for clear character, trust, and humility, well beyond the performance-driven leader who can leave carnage in their path – we have all been there." Barry goes on to say: "It's not always easy to do the right thing – we have all seen this. Being in the trenches, with pressure all around to get the deal done while making the right decisions, takes all of one's experience and abilities. You have to have honor in the game and do the right thing. In the end, character and trust are king."

His story speaks to the essence of stakeholder expectations and the three Ts – truth, trust, and transparency. Leadership is harder than ever before, and this is why leaders need to dig deeper to understand what the unmistakable game changer of stakeholder expectations means. Stakeholder trust is fragile and needs to be nurtured. It is earned every day and is now at the core of a leader's worthiness. It no longer sits outside a leader's mastery of a strategic vision: rather, it must be part of that vision.

Students Are a Critical Stakeholder

It is important to recognize that customer expectations about character and reputation do not just relate to commercially oriented institutions. All sectors have a manifestation of stakeholder expectations – whether in education (through the expectations of students and donors) or health (as it relates to patients and also donors), and so on. They all seek to "trust *and* verify." I hear this firsthand from many students across the University of Toronto. They tell me wonderful stories about how they choose a university, which goes as follows: "Yes, I researched many universities to see which one had the best engineering school. Of course, U of T rated very highly. But it was more than the ratings. I was attracted by the traditions held by U of T engineering, and it also mattered a lot about the values of U of T overall."

Employees Expect Trust!

Marc-André Blanchard describes how trust is so important with leaders in the practice of diplomacy and leadership in embassies and international organizations:

> Diplomacy is about building trust – or rather, building relationships to build trust. Not so different than my experience in running a law firm (especially with 20 per cent of the staff believing the firm is theirs because they're partners). If you have diversity and talent and want to give people space to do their best, then you need a flat organization. And with a flat organization, you can only do things if you have the trust of your partners, your senior managers, the people who will make you successful. Without trust, there's not many tricks in the bag to force things to happen the way you want.

Marc-André's experience as a diplomat with Global Affairs Canada typified those relationships of trust. The staff knew they mattered to him. Leading effectively, he says, starts with experience but requires empathy and trust, with a balance of policy and strategic leadership. Employees, like all stakeholders, expect trust, they just don't wish for it. They expect and look for proof-points of character, of a leader's authenticity and inclusiveness. It's the obligation of leaders to provide this.

As stated in a recent article in the *McKinsey Quarterly*:

> Research has made it clear that tending to multiple stakeholders and managing for the long haul is good for not only stakeholders but also the company. Exposure to customer and stakeholder-related risks are minimized, and new opportunities present themselves. For example, 87 percent of customers say that they will purchase from companies that support what they care about. Ninety-four percent of millennials say that they want their skills to benefit a cause. Sustainable investing has grown 18-fold since 1995. These facts are not new to CEOs, but the COVID-19 pandemic has laid bare the profound interconnectedness between business and the broader world in which they operate. Furthermore, our early research indicates that consumers will be even more committed to social responsibility coming out of the pandemic.[3]

Whether they be customers, employees, students, or shareholders – all are stakeholders with expectations. This is today's reality for leaders. Accordingly, leading well means demonstrating verifiably the three Ts of truth, trust, and transparency to provide certainty of character to the stakeholder. If you need further persuasion of the importance of stakeholder expectations, it is well researched and known that the leader–employee relationship is paramount to retention and, yes, correlated to financial performance results. This is another reason why we call it an unmistakable game changer for leaders and leadership.

CHAPTER THREE

Game Changer #2: The Ever-Changing Workforce and Workplace

The far-reaching impact of this unmistakable game changer – the ever-changing workforce and workplace – was forecasted over a decade ago, in the same period when stakeholder expectations were seriously taking shape and leadership was getting attention everywhere. Statistics and profiles of pending demographic change, immigration, retirements, the increasing generational mix of employees entering the workforce, and the cultural effect of all this were constantly reported. The changing workforce was happening. In fact, it could easily have been foreseen and anticipated from readily available immigration data.

Dramatic Workforce Transformation Was Predicted

Looking back, these facts and data were pointing to a dramatic transformation in our workforce. While organizations worried

FIGURE 6. Changing Workforce

about the aging population and the likely shortage of experience, they were slow to translate what this would mean for leading and leadership capabilities. The concept of leaders needing to adapt and shift mindsets to tune in to such a changing mix of intergenerational and intercultural employees was not top of mind.

The constant references to the workforce transformation and the studies and attention it received, coupled with speculation about millennials dominating the workforce, eventually led to more action. Organizations created and revised human resources practices intended to respond to the different expectations of this new and growing workforce. Statistics of what the workforces would look like by 2020 were updated – and have proven accurate over and over.

75 per cent of millennials are looking for socially responsible employers	Gen Z will comprise **19 per cent** of the workforce by 2025	By 2025 millennials will account for **20 per cent** of promotions while Gen X will account for **10 per cent**

Now, it is not unusual that organizations do not quickly produce strategies for change, especially when disruption is a distance away and medium-to-long term. Focusing on the short term can and does consume leaders – out of necessity and out of a comfort with the familiar. This is what Katie Taylor was alluding to in an earlier chapter when she says she worries about "short-termism."

What Got Us Here Has Changed

Sadly, this new reality of leaders still not having fully adapted to the ever-changing workforce continues to impede their full leadership success and potential. The transformed workforce with its expectations of leaders is here, setting a new paradigm for how leaders lead, energize groups of different mindsets and attributes, and get the best out of teams. Many of today's leaders continue to operate on yesterday's assumptions and the comfort of tried-and-true practices and mindsets.

Even where organizations have implemented innovative practices and talk about the different ways in which leaders need to think, there is still a big lag in the practice by the current C-suite and other leaders. The fact is that the millennials are already in the leadership ranks and having a big influence on shaping the cultural norms; while many of the long-standing leaders are not readily adapting or tuning in to what has transpired. What is now needed is to harness millennial engagement through the discretionary energy of these newer groups in effectively leading the workforce.

The Changing Workplace/Workforce

The pandemic has dramatically heightened this continuing transformation of not only the workforce but also the workplace across all sectors. And while this transformation is not yet clear and while it will continue to unfold, we know that, even within the past two years, many new demands are expected to be placed on leaders' capabilities. The very practice of leader adaptability, strategic agility, and resilience have constantly been called upon in real time. We have witnessed multidimensional and unprecedented challenges, starting with converting to online leading, communicating, strategizing, ensuring clarity, worrying about accountabilities and follow-through – and with a greatly diminished line of sight. Very few centers of work or organizations have been left untouched, thereby causing attempts that were already being contemplated before the pandemic became a reality to be renewed.

Leadership Is *Not* Timeless

Above all, what this teaches us is that leadership is *not* timeless. What got us to here in the past has changed and continues to change in unprecedented ways. This very different workforce needs different consideration. Leaders have to open their minds; they have to think and lead differently. That is why leadership cannot be timeless. Instead, it must relate to the diversity of age, gender, race, and cultural differences that comprise the workforce of today and of the future. And that workforce expects a more open-minded approach by leaders. The workers want to be listened to, not just talked to. They expect leaders to tell them the "why" of things and allow them to question the status quo.

Engaging Employees Is Harder and Solutions Have Become More Complex

Tiff Macklem captures the importance of team motivation and engagement with this ever-changing workforce – and the dilemmas encountered by leaders when people around them are not buying in to a new vision. "If you get people excited about the 'why,' they'll give you all they've got. From there, proceed to the 'who' – that is, build the team around you, using the value of diversity of thought and approach to get the best advice possible. Then, thirdly, decide on the 'what' – the action resulting from the decision taken, now collectively executed by the team acting as one." But what happens if the people around you are not fully sharing the vision, the goals, and the common endeavor? This may seem like a real problem, although as Tiff notes, it is in fact sometimes easier to fix than one would think. He puts it this way: "It begins with how you relate to people. Are you recognizing diversity in people? While this may seem obvious, it didn't come naturally to me when I was a first-time manager and tended to assume that others were just like me. I found I needed to talk differently to some people than others – all part of recognizing diversity."

Realizing just how valuable this was in achieving goals together was a major step for Tiff, not only in self-awareness but also in getting to the best decisions with the support of the team. It taught him the real value of inclusion and diversity. It also taught him the value of *spirited collaboration* and how to get the best from it:

> Some people are comfortable with tension and competing ideas; they can accept a certain degree of conflict with different views. Others cannot; they respond differently, sometimes with anxiety. As a leader, you have to be comfortable with tension among your senior executives – and not cut it off too soon. And you must help others get comfortable with a healthy degree of creative tension. Otherwise, you miss the full value of diverse thought processes and what they were weighing to get to their recommendations (with which one might not agree).

In other words, help your team enjoy spirited collaboration by building trust – in you and in the process.

Leading through Dissent

Janice Gross Stein arrives at the topic of inclusion and dissent from another perspective, finding in recent international crises and disruptions a common theme:

> What lies at basis of these crises? Inclusion. It's all about inclusion. Each crisis required the capacity to think beyond one's own borders, to connect local circumstances to a larger context. Inclusivity goes beyond gender balance, beyond racial justice: it is all-encompassing for the future. Moreover, if we are seriously committed to inclusion, we will have to become more comfortable with disagreement and conflict at the table. It is a challenge to orthodoxy. That is why we need leaders who can handle well-managed conflict and discussion

and don't run from it, as is often done in boardrooms through the "absence of dissent." Knowing how to lead a group through dissent may be the most important attribute for leadership. In fact, inclusivity requires tolerating dissent.

She further notes that, while it may be too soon to draw or predict anything from the COVID-19 crisis, leadership will be upended for sure. Not only will leaders need to be open-minded to see and understand the longer-term impact but they will also need agility to navigate complexity and to understand how complex the journey from A to B can be. And this means intentionality. As Janice says, leaders "need to be inclusive, yes, but not at the expense of being intentional."

Intention: Beyond Instinct

As both Janice and Tiff point out, the role of leaders is to inspire, empower, and engage their teams and other groups in order to harness energy and get real engagement and alignment. Today's context has pushed leaders to stay tuned to the changing workforce. This, though, requires a much more *intentional* and deliberate way of leading. Being instinctive and acting only on past successes is just not enough to lead a dramatically transformed workforce. And now, as we move through the early 2020s, this workforce reality is one of the three most challenging unmistakable game changers for leaders – namely, becoming even more attuned to the people for whom they have the responsibility of inspiring and engaging.

Consider the pandemic's most current demand on such critical analyses and pressing judgments that leaders face, such as when and how their employees, students, and all relevant populations under their stewardship should return to work, the classroom, and other related places. Clearly, leaders have never had to tackle such a critical call. It would therefore be helpful to have attitudes that are really tuned in to the workforce and to the changing expectations in order to minimize the chances of getting this wrong.

Through the many past and present disruptions, which began with the generational influx, the personal experiences and journeys of so many leaders have been to adapt and renew – and today one thing we know is that leaders need to adapt to very different expectations pervading our workforce. Employee groups look for consistency in their workplace, in the decisions made by leaders, and in their own personal values around respect and inclusion. Leaders need to empathize with this. This does not mean that leaders are expected to feed employees everything they want. Rather, the leader's job is to know what motivates and inspires – and then be able to do the best thing for the larger good. Leadership is hard, but it has never been more important.

Post-Pandemic: New Layers of Challenges

Now, as the post-pandemic environment evolves and takes shape, there will be new layers of challenges for leaders who will face new issues for both the workforce and the way in which employees work. The effectiveness of leaders will be tested in multiple ways. In particular, the engagement of employees will be increasingly harder to obtain. As work itself transforms, employees will demand greater empowerment. The workplace hybrid manner of working will challenge the traditional methods of engaging employees. Other complexities will mount from the layers of data, trends, and stories from the pandemic. This all points to the focus on harnessing human potential and recognizing it as our greatest untapped asset. Within this changing context, striving for productivity will take on new meanings. This is playing out now as we grapple with the best way to lead with hybrid work models. By using available technologies to automate dull, repetitive activities, we can elevate the human elements that bring out more innovative practices, *not* replace people. Employees want greater autonomy, more choice, and more flexibility to individualize their work experiences according to the way they live their lives.

While this is promising, we are seeing that employee uncertainty and demands for empowerment are more complex than ever. Leaders are facing employees with different frames of mind – ranging from exhaustion, feeling overworked, and feeling ambivalent about what is best for them. At the same time, leaders themselves are experiencing some of the same anxieties, although, according to a 2021 Deloitte report on leadership, leaders are faring better at grappling with the demands.[1] As the ever-changing workplace and workforce game changer continues to intensify, we gain hope for the ongoing renewal of leaders' adaptability – even as inspiring others continues to get harder.

Remote-hybrid models can work. We know that in 2021, 32 per cent of all employees worldwide were represented by remote workers, compared with 17 per cent in 2019.[2]

My conversation with Marc André began and closed with his statement, "Leadership is the capability to motivate and inspire your team." He believes that today's employees want to see leaders who are generous, open, trustworthy, and, above all, honest with them. Leadership and team experiences are closely intertwined, regardless of whether one is in the private or the public sector – as he knows full well, having been a leader in both. As we will see later in chapter 8, Marc André acknowledges that leading in Global Affairs Canada can be different than leading in a private corporation. However, one can achieve success in both if the leader is intentional and deliberate. This is the unifying factor of leadership across sectors.

Unmistakable game changer #2 – the ever-changing workforce and workplace – confirms that what got leaders to their current levels of success won't necessarily keep them here. The multigenerational and multicultural mix of talent no doubt brings a richness that leaders can and need to capture and utilize. It means that leaders who are renewing their approaches are creating intentionally deliberate pathways toward far greater alignment through diversity and inclusiveness. While navigating remote work and hybrid models, they are bringing teams together, enabling cross-boundary discussions, and encouraging expressions of dissent, with the outcome being better collaboration. All of which is based on spirited debate rather than on the more typically used approach of gaining consensus through an echo chamber that is void of dissent.

Making sense of and embracing the intense differences and workplace shifts occurring in today's workforce can help open the door to success. In fact, we can say that leadership success depends on it.

CHAPTER FOUR

Game Changer #3: Short-Lived Strategies and Digital Dominance

When leaders are being discussed in the boardroom or when organizations are lagging and doubts arise about the leader's effectiveness and suitability to lead in current times, the concerns always land on one of three unmistakable game changers – increased stakeholder expectations or the ever-changing workforce and workplace.

In this chapter, we explore the third unmistakable game changer – short-lived strategies and digital dominance. It used to be that strategy and its effectiveness dominated in the boardroom. Then the ethics, values, and principles of an organization became the focus. Most recently, the people side of leading has been getting more attention. Now, we are also circling back to explore the implications of what *strategy* means in today's environment and how it impacts a leader's effectiveness.

It might be helpful to take a snapshot of how strategy has been approached and conceived over time. This is the basis of why adapting to today's needs is highly challenging for many leaders and why organizations in many sectors are seen to be struggling from time to time. The path to developing strategy used to

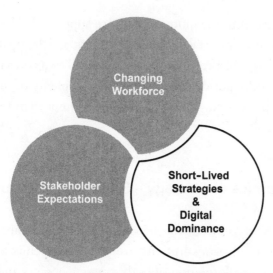

FIGURE 7. Short-Lived Strategies and Digital Dominance

involve a variety of frameworks by which to present the strategy, followed by periodic updates or a review after four to five years. Sometimes annual strategy updates were done. Indeed, many organizations might not even have had an explicitly stated strategy; or, if they did, it may have been a "SPOT" (strategic plan on the shelf). The belief that strategies should have a longer life span lingers on, even amidst much chatter about the uncertain world in which we live.

In his recent article in the *Harvard Business Review*,[1] David Collis holds that the days of "once and done" strategy preparation are over. "The CEO's job of crafting a strategy that creates and captures value and keeps realizing it over time ... has never been harder." He states that CEOs often underestimate how much new technologies and business models can increase the value provided to customers. In chapter 1, Ron Farmer, a longtime expert on the ins and outs of strategy, described the pressure on leaders to articulate a strategic vision almost from the moment they are appointed: "Today, organizations, boards and stakeholders have less and less patience, and leadership must be prepared for and respond to a constant sense of urgency." No longer do leaders have or take plenty of time to get a strategy in place. Being bolder will be more important than ever; so too, speed and agility.

The Dynamics of Strategy – Seeing around Corners

We have clearly moved well beyond the days of general strategic updates. Survival of institutions everywhere depends on constant renewal and transformation of both strategic choices and operating models. The constant and continuing disruptions that have played out in this last decade are simply rendering many (even major) strategies outdated or defunct. No wonder strategy fits the criteria of being an unmistakable game changer with which leaders have to contend. Being strategically agile is the number one requirement. Leaders are having to demonstrate, and live with the fact, that strategy is totally dynamic and not at all static. A leader locked into the tried and true of yesterday and being unable to let go is following a recipe for failure and obsolescence.

In our conversations, Tiff Macklem talks about strategic agility in preparing for the inevitable choppy waters that all leaders encounter when they're at the helm. What will be its impact across society, across the economy, over the next months and years? What this means is that leaders have to continue thinking ahead, even in the midst of battling a crisis. And that means, according to Tiff, "A leader has to carve out a staff group to start thinking about the next problems and preparing for them."

Underlying the mindset of "holding on" and not letting go of favored strategies is the assumption – long held by CEOs and other leaders – that these strategies are proprietary and therefore "safe" for a while longer. This once gave the leaders relief as they focused on executing the present, even when, in their minds and hearts, they likely knew the strategy would prove to be suboptimal. It is not easy to change and it is even harder to let go of a tried-and-true familiar strategy. We see this over and over.

Execution Does Matter, while Seeing around Corners

Of course, we know it is always true that execution is even more critical than how brilliant the strategy is itself. However, leaders need to be reminded that strategy is also market-based. It depends on ongoing analysis and fast action. It is about leaders "seeing around corners" at all times. This is very hard in a harsh environment; but we must remember that unpredictable situations are magnets for inaction. Strategy is not proprietary. It does not wait for leaders.

This can be seen more than ever today with the escalation of digitalization and its dominance on strategy renewal. Digitalization is quickly teaching leaders that strategy is not just grounded in experience and wisdom – it is now dependent on market intelligence and being tuned into market volatility. Strategy is not just about one's past experience nor is it about one's intelligence (IQ); rather, it's about analysis, adjusting, and action (the "three As" of strategy) in response to changing contexts and disruption.

Digitalization Accelerates

As we consider the pandemic's implications for shaping strategy, we can see that it has accelerated the adoption of digitalization within organizations, and it is digitalization that will continue to impact the pace by which organizations move and succeed. The acceleration of digitalization poses the biggest questions about past assumptions and about the leader's agility, even in the most advanced and successful institutions. We know we have been slow to embrace and adapt to the technologies and their underpinning of the move to digital enablers. This is true across all industries. It is estimated, for instance, that what we once did in two years was surpassed in two months during COVID-19. While this is impressive by any measure, it does shine a light on the fact that senior leaders themselves (not unlike some of the larger workforce) are slower to learn how to embrace the true value and necessity of driving strategy by using the digitalization lens. Any strategic differences we detect today in an organization's success reflect the level of proficiency and use of technology capabilities.

This reinforces the fact that leadership capabilities need to catch up real fast, just as people strategies have done by including technology mandates to advance the talent pipelines of emerging leaders. It means that one of the most important obligations facing leaders at all times, and especially in these times, is their own self-renewal and the development of others (mentoring). John Chambers, former CEO of Cisco, is one of the foremost pioneers in embracing technology and predicting the explosion of growth in technology devices and the dominance of digital use. He has for a long time spoken of the predicted multiples of growth in devices and their uses and applications. This now has become evident as we examine the differences between those organizations that are adapting and seizing the movement and those struggling or failing because of their resistance or complacency. It is true across all sectors, regardless of size and complexity, including banks, hospitals, and universities.

Darryl White speaks of the importance of developing digital fluency and adapting to new ways:

We made a choice at the bank to become a "digital first" company. You have to make clear choices on digital and establish an inflection point. There have been other inflection points that set the stage. Twenty-five years ago, it was about scale and distribution channels like the Internet. Then came user experience through technology tools. After that, ten years ago, it was internal structure, what does the "architecture" of your company need to look like to produce the most efficient outcome for your cost structure? Now, with artificial intelligence, machine learning, quantum computing, it's more about efficiency and speed, about pattern recognition to drive outcomes. That's the spectrum we're all on today.

Embracing Technology

Meric Gertler offers examples of how COVID-19 influenced leadership and technology adoption at the University of Toronto:

How we handled COVID-19 is an interesting story. We successfully pivoted 6,000 courses over a weekend back in March 2020 – a remarkable achievement. Now we're improving the quality of teaching and learning in a virtual mode. A whole cohort of faculty had to learn these things overnight. We've moved farther in the last year than ever before in using Internet platforms and virtual teaching technologies. Effective virtual teaching courses have been greatly subscribed to by faculty.

It is one thing to adopt the technology and another thing to prepare for its continued use, expansion, and upgrade. Even more strategic is the preparation for the next crisis – as evidenced by the planning, implementation, and exercise of a crisis management plan based on the distribution and use of digital technology. Meric describes what they did:

Another part of the story is the crisis management plan we developed before COVID-19. It gave us a place to start when the pandemic struck and a state of emergency was declared. We set up a crisis center and pulled in people from all over in the university with important skill sets, thereby creating a cross-functional team. The team is still in place, adjusted and adapted now to recovery planning. Do we need to institutionalize this capacity, if not preserve it intact, post–COVID-19, given how challenging it was to set up and operate? We must also realize that, as the pandemic continues, people become "more brittle." We've asked them to pivot so many times, they're running out of capacity to do so. How do we maintain that level of agility over time? This is what keeps me up at night.

Adaptability plus Agility

Meric's story conveys many of the themes leaders encounter as they navigate uncertainty and uncharted waters. It all boils down to having good strategic agility. But good strategic agility is not the same as personal adaptability. Instead, it means keeping the foundations that you've created and inspiring others to do the same. Otherwise, atrophy starts to set in and the gains fade. In other words, how do leaders retain the momentum, the openness, and willingness to embrace change? How do they foster dynamism within their organizations? What incentives and structures are needed? In response to such questions, Meric has created an "architecture of institutional initiatives built around problems." As he describes it: "There are no barriers to participation. Rather, it's about solving problems, that is, harnessing technology for social benefit, green energy, socioeconomic challenges. We've created a venture fund within the university to provide 'carrots of incentive' with lots of investments in little projects. It's a revolutionary approach for the university world."

FIGURE 8. The Three Unmistakable Game Changers

The unmistakable game changer of short-lived strategies and digital dominance makes leading well so much harder. It requires three key steps: (a) grasping the potential of available technologies and making sense of them before others already outrun you, (b) adjusting or letting go of current strategies, and (c) acting with courage and fortitude to move it all forward, even in the face of adversity and resistance. It clearly confirms that leading with intention has become a must.

The Three Game Changers Intertwine

This brings us back to the unmistakable game changer of the ever-changing workforce and workplace, in which leaders are accountable for inspiring, leading, and energizing. Similarly, it brings us back to the unmistakable game changer of increased stakeholder expectations, with the trust and character imperatives that are table stakes for success. Understanding the human impact of technology will change much for leading. It will certainly challenge many leaders. Digitalization (on its own) has been stated to cause 30 to 40 per cent of leaders to struggle significantly. In fact, leaders are often replaced because of their inability or unwillingness to adapt and lead talent well enough through these times. According to John Chambers, leading people will be even more challenging as organizations move to digital enablers.

The strategies chosen by leaders for their organizations, the speed by which they move, how they handle all the dynamics of change, the short shelf life and the technological implications of their strategies – these will push for renewed leader capabilities. We see the cost side of this being embraced: "Talent poses a perennial challenge to companies that are transforming their business through digital and technology. As organizations make their plans for filling critical talent gaps in technology, from the board to the front line, the results suggest that there is no silver bullet to filling skill gaps. Top economic performers report a greater reliance in hiring new employees. At other companies, respondents report an equal focus on hiring and retraining their current people, and the two groups rely equally on partnering or contracting."[2]

Leadership development and renewal will therefore need to keep pace or risk losing opportunities for success. Personal adaptability, strategic agility, and resilience will all have to be part of leaders' profiles now. Not unlike a decade ago, when we saw so many turning points for leaders and many innovative and bold moves, this is now a more critical time to reset, renew, and transform what is possible from them.

From External Disruptions to Internal Beliefs

Throughout part 1, we explored some of the core reasons why leadership has never been more important and why it is hard to lead well. The focus on each of the three unmistakable game changers largely related to the *external disruptions* across the landscape that are affecting all sectors and institutions in some dramatic way. Such disruptions are beyond any one organization's control, but it behooves each to grasp, embrace, and respond to them – and to be held accountable.

Next, in part 2, this effort to make sense continues with the focus on the individual leader. We will examine the false confidence a leader gets from long-held beliefs about leadership – in particular, (1) that leadership is timeless (it's not); (2) that leaders are expected to have all the answers (not possible); (3) that leaders are chosen based on past "high" performance and less on how they might lead for today (flawed); and (4) the age-old assumption that softer skills (or human skills) inevitably come with time and so they can be forgotten or given less priority (also flawed).

PART TWO

Long-Held Beliefs, Myths, and
Habits – Challenges to Leaders'
Success

CHAPTER FIVE

Dispelling Myths Takes Energy and Courage

The thought manifests itself as the word. The word manifests itself as the deed. The deed develops into habit. The habit hardens into character.

A philosopher named Anonymous

Our beliefs of today are grounded in our thoughts of yesterday and our actions are driven by our beliefs. Beliefs are powerful but we can own them – and we can change them. It's up to us! Much is now written about the impact of one's *mindset*. Often heard is "Does John have an open mindset or an inflexible mindset or a closed mindset?" Those writings give meaning and substance to the simple truth that how we think – and what we assume or believe – drive how a leader will lead. How leaders lead is grounded in firmly held beliefs and assumptions.

What leaders believe matters and it is truly up to them. Leaders own how they think. They can change it if they have the desire and the courage to try and the fortitude to stay the course. This is central to whether a leader is adapting or staying locked into yesterday's assumptions. Some leaders do think narrowly; some think negatively about life's possibilities; others think optimistically about possibilities. Many think honorably all the time, whereas some do not; some think with knowledge and fact while others think purely in opinion.

Leaders Can Choose Their Mindset

It is my firm view that beliefs and mindsets can be changed. People (leaders included) have control over them. Leaders can choose how they think; it is a right, although it has consequences – both positive and negative. Leaders own the impact and the consequences! This is the difference between using pure instinct to lead and *intentional leading*.

Darryl White describes his own move from instinctive to intentional leading as an evolution. At first, he was totally instinctual – he worked in his given environment, took what came, dealt with it, and moved on. Modern management ideas like templates and playbooks seemed unnecessary, and they made him resistant. So, when did the penny finally drop and he knew he had to renew his thinking? His answer: "When I realized my challenge as a leader 'was not to lead me.' It was to lead others – and they are different than me. This meant something more than just getting up every day, going to work, generally winging it." He realized he needed an "intentional map."

Today, Darryl starts all conversations with "intentionality," beginning with a reaffirmation of the organization's values and what's most important. He speaks of a map, in which diversity, empathy, and purpose constitute the map's destinations. Then he identifies the means (or "levers") by which one gets to the destination. "Everything must be brought back to the map. Why? People have a habit of going off and doing their own thing, some want to be left alone, others need direction and purpose. It is important to motivate them all. That's why you rehearse the map every time. Furthermore, the map has to look and feel the same for everyone: we need to speak a common language around it." It is here that intentional leadership meets strategy. Darryl says he would have failed if he hadn't brought in some kind of structure to help him as well as others focus on the important things. With so many distractions these days, we keep well-grounded by asking, Is it on the map or not?

Beliefs and Habits Inform How We Lead

My own learnings grew profoundly when I considered how my beliefs and therefore habits and practices were informing how I was leading. When I began to question my mindset on particular topics or issues, I could see why I was not always as effective as I wanted to be. It clarified how I could increase the positive impact that I was striving for as a leader wanting to accomplish many things across many sectors. One of the exercises I now have in my class at the Rotman School of Management is to suggest to leaders that before any meeting and before any class discussion they pause and consider the following questions, "What do I believe about this issue? What is my true mindset toward it? Is it closed or already shaped?" This little exercise is no more than pausing to reflect and checking one's own stance. What does a leader have to lose? The worst that can happen is that they will learn something that is possibly helpful.

The Story of Walter
I once worked with a CEO (Walter) who excelled at everything. It didn't seem to matter to him that his industry had become highly volatile with competition tougher

and harsher, because his ability to adapt and renew his capabilities was staggering. What was his recipe? One day we met in my advisory capacity and reflected on his most recent impacts.[1] Walter asked for my views on his leadership, given that I'd observed and studied it over time. My first characterization was about his mindset – his ability to reflect on the beliefs governing his decisions and always establishing intention over instinct. He was a living example of what the Anonymous philosopher described at the beginning of this chapter. As Walter phrased it: "We should watch our thoughts with great care," adding that we should "let our thoughts stem from a place of concern for all." He reinforced this thoughtful and values-based leadership approach with the practices of generosity, even-handedness, and empathy. Moreover, his approach was an antidote to the blind spots that many leaders are sometimes unaware they have, due to outdated mindsets and beliefs. It allowed him to check consciously for blind spots and then, also consciously, to strive to change them.

What brought leaders here will not keep them here. There's a limited shelf life and a context that changes all the time. Intention, reflection, feedback, and a willingness to understand or rethink practices are all matters of leadership, combined with the curiosity, courage, and energy to let go of ideas and approaches that have outlasted their "best by" date. Yet, as I have discovered in the work leading up to the Big 8 and from hundreds of interactions with leaders in classes, most leaders do not pause or take time to question their beliefs, their biases, or their stance on particular ways of leading. They stay guided by them repeatedly, even over years in the midst of all the game changers and disruptions. Their fixed mindset of "once a good leader, always a good leader" drives their thinking, their conversation, their actions, and, of course, the kind of impact they have.

The enlightening book *Mindset: The New Psychology of Success* by Carol S. Dweck is masterful at delving into the whys and hows of the workings of one's mindset. It can be a powerful tool in a leader's efforts to be intentional and more adaptable. Dweck's many explanations and her making sense of mindset and learning are inspirational and helpful. She suggests that for champions to exist and persist, they must believe in and understand that natural ability and talent are helpful, but more important is mindset being open to the concept of learning as well as failure.[2] In the case of Walter, who was a champion in many ways, he also avoided what Dweck refers to as "CEO disease" – that is, "reigning from the top of a pedestal." Walter had a mindset of striving to be worthy of being a leader.

During this work I have derived the *four most common false beliefs* that help to make sense of why leadership is harder. I call this the second perspective.[3] This perspective focuses on leaders' individual mindsets and beliefs and how these can lift up, or hinder, their aspired journey toward leading well. Here are the four false beliefs impeding one's success as a leader:

1. Leadership is timeless: once a great leader, always a great leader. (Not true!)
2. Softer skills will improve, just give them time. (Not true!)
3. High performance equals high potential for leadership. (Not true!)
4. Mentors are important mostly for lower levels in leading. (Not true!)

These four false beliefs are not the only ones, of course. There are others. But these four are common to many leaders' mindsets.

There is no escaping their existence and the extent to which leaders can be suboptimal because of them. The impact and false confidence imbued by these four false beliefs appear even in leaders who are seemingly leading well. In others, it happens over a longer period, sometimes subtly, and leaders are often oblivious to it. But these four beliefs are known, as I have witnessed unfortunately, to cause a leader's derailment. So now, let's look at each of the false beliefs.

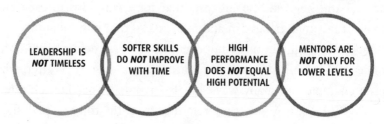

FIGURE 9. False Beliefs of Leaders

CHAPTER SIX

Leadership Is Not Timeless – It Has a Shelf Life

The significant problems we face cannot be solved at the same level of thinking we were at, before they were created.

Albert Einstein

Know Your Impact

There is no lasting formula for leadership. Yes, for decades we have questioned, argued, and declared opinions about whether leadership is timeless (or not). Many leaders arrived at the pinnacle thinking, then believing, that once we became a good leader, we would stay a good leader. For most who lead, it is only much later that the flaws in this assumption start to show, but not always to everyone. The struggles that leaders face from time to time are subtle and, over time, they steadily weaken the realization that the "once a good leader" mindset has a limited shelf life. What got you here has changed.

Impacts matter. Positive impacts on others are at the heart of great leadership. Leaders have many goals and achievements; different things are important at various stages of their career – money, power, title, and so on. But at the end of the day, for those leaders who inspire others, making a positive impact is the essence of success.

Unrealized Potential

Encountering situations where leadership potential and talent are not realized and in fact are wasted has been among my saddest experiences. This is especially so when it is mostly because of a lack of self-renewal; when leaders have been imprisoned by a fixed mindset or belief that learning slows or stops once they reach successful leadership. I see the promise of impactful careers, and often personal hopes, shattered and so often unfilled.

For others, they have jettisoned such imprisoning mindsets. Great leadership is all about lifelong learning. It does not stop. Katie Taylor shows us what this means. "We are products of our own experiences – so where we start cannot be anywhere near where we are later on or in our 'experienced years.' Leadership requires lifelong learning, not just about things but about yourself." Katie knew from an early age that she was a competitor, striving for the best marks, the first in the family to go to university. When she was growing up, professionals and people in business were men. Women went into teaching and nursing. "However, I'd always been an organizer of people – getting events going, staging plays, playing on sports teams in high school, trying to egg people on to greater effort. Maybe this would be possible in the world of business? It still took ten years or so to realize this ambition and get out of small-town thinking."

Rueful Yearning

What often comes through when I speak with some senior executives is a reflection, almost a rueful yearning, about how knowing and understanding things earlier would have helped them tremendously throughout their leadership journey. Had they acquired such understanding, they feel they would have been even better leaders having even greater impact. I see them as leaders who reflect and care about their impact and how they did – or did not – lead. But sometimes it's too late.

Such ruminations about what might have been or could have been better reinforces my strong contention that leadership is all about self-renewal and lifelong learning. We are often led to believe that, when leadership is generally successful over a long period, it must be timeless, eternal. This is the result of confusion. While it is true that a person can be born with natural abilities for leading and that this can take them far on the leadership journey, it will, however, not be enough to keep that person there. To believe that "leaders are born" is to suggest that innate abilities and instinct will suffice to lead successfully and well. But with so much change around us that is truly transforming, how can this be? Einstein's quote at the beginning of the chapter says it well.

Leadership Is Dynamic

What got us here, whether naturally or from many learned capabilities, is fueled by *intention*. Leadership is dynamic; it is not static. It is driven by the changing context that is continuously shaped by our changing landscapes and further propelled by a leader's own choice about renewal and the dispelling of long-held beliefs. And an important part of renewal is that leadership is both learned and is strengthened through lifelong learning.

FIGURE 10. Connections Build

How leaders continue to learn is a fundamental thread running through Janice Gross Stein's own work on leadership. "Having seen many styles of leadership across government, politics, and businesses, what emerges as the key determinant is context. Leaders make a big mistake if they become overly comfortable in a context because they're pretty good at it. The result? Less awareness and sensitivity to what is changing around them."

Janice then connects learning with change and leadership:

There are two types of change. One is change within the broad boundaries of what people know and within the framework of that which brought people to leadership. That's a problem, but not so bad as number two – when the context changes. "We will build back" is uncomfortable and deeply flawed about what the leadership challenges will be in the future. Take COVID-19, for example. It has changed the context entirely. Leaders advocating a return to "normalcy" are not preparing themselves or their constituency for the future. Identifying whether deep and irrevocable change is happening is one of the most significant challenges a leader must face. Those who succeed are sensitive to qualitative change.

A turning point is reached when leaders realize change is happening and they need different skills and different people around them. Look at the fundamental mindset of the individual. Is there a comfort level with the tried and true, an inability to imagine beyond the status quo? The answer will reflect a leader's intelligence, mindset, emotional makeup, upbringing. Breaking the comfort mindset is key to getting through to a new level. However, it can be blocked by fear of uncertainty and lack of confidence that you have a deep enough understanding of the change to cope with new circumstances.

We see everywhere a constant yearning for better leadership. Today, it is sought more forcefully than ever. Boards and governments are increasing their attention for sure, but our entire society and all its citizens are tuned in to, more than ever, the quality of leading around them. The disruptions all relate to their well-being and demonstrate notions of what leaders are accountable for. Leaders are in the spotlight. People are paying attention and questioning what they see.

Call to Action: Beyond Past Paradigms

This reality leads to the frequently asked questions: Can leadership be learned? Can it be taught? It is certainly a call to action to start thinking differently about how best to lead and whether one's own practices are meeting the test. The spotlight on leadership is now also revealing a much greater weight being placed on very specific skills and behaviors. Those had not been as explicit in our past paradigms of what made up the critical capabilities, when most leaders moved through their own leadership journeys.

Such lessons in leadership didn't get taught in our MBA and other advanced programs, even though, for multiple reasons, those programs have deservedly been regarded among the best in choosing and placing potential leaders. It begs the question whether we have sometimes placed too much reliability on the power of the MBA and such formal teachings and not enough on deliberate, just-in-time leadership self-renewal.

For example, Roger Martin, former dean of the Rotman School of Management and one of my most admired leaders, has referred to the idea that some MBA students/holders can often have an over-developed sense of power in the analytical models they learned and an underdeveloped sense of their limitations for leadership success in handling the complexities seen in today's disruptive times.

Professors have cautioned us about overreliance on purely formal education, for managing and leading well, pointing out that, while one does acquire functional tools and understanding in several disciplines – economics, marketing, finance, accounting – that's all very well, but one's training in the capacity for managing/leading is more limited. A quote by Henry Mintzberg expresses this thought well: "Leadership is like swimming, it cannot be learned by reading about it."

The reality, of course, is that formal education is essential for today's complexity. It is table stakes and extremely valuable – but no longer *enough* because it is most often done in case study and classroom-like settings where the problem is solved with single right answers. However, today's societal as well as all leadership issues are, regardless of sector, much more varied and complex and much more unpredictable. Fixed mindsets and static renewal can suppress this. The hold on leadership is not timeless. For these and many other reasons, even our ideal role models will not remain at the same level of excellence without their own renewal; they too can be subject to the same limitations.

The Lifelong Learners

Where does the ability or inclination to renew come from? To admit that one might be unequipped but can quickly learn in a just-in-time manner is an important attribute to recognize. For Mary Anne Chambers, this ability "comes from an openness to being a lifelong learner, a practiced approach to ensuring one is equipped for the new or different responsibility and willing to put in the energy." A good example of Mary Anne's practiced approach to learning is seen in the director role she accepted on a hospital board. Deeply committed and wanting to be a good and conscientious contributor, she immediately dug deeply into hospital policy to learn all she could in a deliberate and intentional way. Not only did she serve the board and the hospital very well through such dedication and leadership; within a year she was appointed as the board's vice-chair.

Mary Anne's example shows us clearly that leadership is never timeless or purely instinctive. It is learned, renewed, and learned in a continuous cycle. The belief that "once you become an accomplished leader, you'll always be a good leader" is flawed and harmful. It can erode one's impact! What got us here won't keep us here. Running a marathon at an attractive speed does not make for a lifetime ability of running well. Leading is about agility and is not unlike our muscles, which will weaken with time if not constantly maintained and kept flexible.

CHAPTER SEVEN

Softer Skills Do Not Improve with Just Time

How often have you heard others say the following or also thought yourself along similar lines? "This person is being chosen for this significant leadership position and we have every confidence they will succeed, given previous success and a good track record of performance results in most instances. Now, we know this position will be a stretch on the softer skills side, but we think that's not a showstopper – those will improve with time, after a few months in the role."

The Consequence of Role-Modeling

This assumption – that time will fix the softer skill situation – has been one of the most strongly held beliefs, as well as frequently practiced, when choosing leaders. Certainly, it is one of the biggest causes of leaders stumbling, struggling, or even failing eventually. At the same time, the unintended but negative consequences of a leader's lack of empathy, communication, and role-modeling are dramatic and harmful. A leader's subordinates, peers, customers, and colleagues are always affected. This potentially negative impact or harm can have long-lasting influence. It reflects poor role-modeling – one of the central obligations for leaders.

Leaders don't realize, or they underestimate, the way in which they are observed and judged by subordinates and all those around them. In fact, when I discuss this with leaders, they are amazed at the influence they have. My own story on this goes back to when I was promoted to executive vice-president at the Bank of Montreal (BMO) – this was over twenty years ago at a time when such positions were rare and especially so for women. The day my appointment was announced, I received 104 emails from many people across the bank, many of whom I did not know personally, but they had had some exposure to me. Those emails were more than congratulations – the majority of well-wishers had literally expressed why, in their mind, I deserved the promotion and recognition. I was shocked by the detail of their observations and the definitive nature of why those traits and actions they observed were so important. Many of their comments and observations were surprising to me. I had not realized that I had been displaying such (positive, in this case) behaviors.

It was one of my biggest lessons learned and some of the most impactful feedback I have had in my entire career. People watch everything you do as a leader and take away positive or negative re-actions. It is enormously influential to the growth and development of others. Of course, I did not receive any emails from those who might have observed the behaviors that I would need to improve and which would be very critical to my growth, and this taught me to seek such feedback as I went forward.

This experience reminds me of the well-known expression often attributed to the poet Maya Angelou: "People will forget what you said, people will forget what you did, but people will never forget how you made them feel." My advice to others on role-modeling is to really care about your impact on others. Words matter! It's another important reason why leaders need to be reflective and intentional and not act on pure instinct. Greatness in leaders is measured by their positive impact, no matter what other success they can claim. Role-modeling happens through the stories leaders tell, the questions they ask, and the manner in which they connect with others every day.

Words Matter a Lot!

Darryl White agrees that words matter. As he says: "That light went on a while back. Most things in our lives these days are recorded. Awareness of this is a characteristic of leadership – you can use it as an upside. But ignore it and there can be a real downside. I found that even a simple aside can be interpreted as a strong value statement by people who don't know you. You have to realize the influence you have – not just as CEO but also along the way of your leadership journey." It is therefore well to be reminded that leadership is a privilege and has serious responsibility. It is about being trusted to guide others, to add value to their learnings, and to earn their trust and respect. It is not just a rite of passage for those who are entrusted with leadership. Darryl also tells a story of a situation where he, as the boss, decided for a cheaper car for practical family reasons. When that purchase become known by employees, the perception of it was such that gossip began to go round suggesting that the boss's "downgrading" of his car meant that company bonuses would therefore also be down that year. As Darryl says about this anecdote: "People watch so much more of what a leader portrays than anyone realizes."

Widespread Harm

For leaders who don't make softer skills a top priority, some reflection on the Maya Angelou quote and hearing stories from so many other leaders' experiences should jolt them into a serious and intentional approach to prioritizing those skills. It is all about self-awareness. Statements describing someone as having sharp elbows, but gets the job done – or "a person's bark is worse than their bite, but they get the job done; meanwhile the rough edges will wear off" – are common judgments used to suggest that the softer skills are of lesser importance. Yet we need to be aware of whether or not we are subscribing to that assumption when selecting candidates to lead or when we do our own self-assessment for improvement. There is also a latent assumption that softer skills are a sign of weakness; or that, if such skills are needed in a leadership position, they will come with time and therefore there is no need to be concerned. But we've just pointed out that a leader's words and comportment matter. The harm done when human situations are messed up due to the toleration of someone's "sharp elbows" or "barks that are worse than their bite" can have long-lasting damage. Perfection in producing spreadsheets does not compensate for a lack of the softer skills.

Practices Are Improving

Albeit more slowly than we would wish, leadership practice is improving, as the leadership pendulum shifts toward making the softer skills a priority. Evidence that this is being recognized is increasing across all sectors. Expectations for leaders to be empathetic, compassionate, and good listeners and communicators are now more explicitly discussed and are becoming mandatory, with clear evidence of past and current practices being valued. The long-held belief that those skills will improve with time, without further deliberate adjustment by the leader, is known to be flawed. It is a common blind spot that silently erodes a leader's effectiveness. Leaders with mediocre softer skills will drift into an ineffective leadership. And what a shame this is! Such leaders often have all the technical, analytical, and strategic abilities that can mask this shortcoming. But it does not compensate for how much better they could lead and how much more positive an impact they could have both on their organization and on all those around them if they exercised better softer skills. This is especially true for a leader's direct subordinates whose experiences of positive impacts could be paramount to their development and success.

Latent Self-Awareness

Self-awareness and learning to lead are essential here, as testified to by a high-potential leader attending one of my executive leadership classes whom we will call Mary. Mary had encountered failure while working on a pivotal project in her career goals. This was a big setback for her at the time. But then she reflected on what it meant for her development as a leader. "Wow, I didn't learn this in business school. I guess what got me here in terms of higher grades and analytics won't get me to the next level of real leading. I want to lead well. I now see that being a good leader is not just about me and who I am, and what I can do or just being smart – it's about how I impact others that will be important. It's about how I think about others and how to lead and inspire this." So, the setback wasn't the end of the story for her; nor the end of her career aspirations. She reflected and learned something vital about leadership.

IQ – EQ – DQ

Mary's story is now more commonly heard as the prominence of softer skills is exposed and regarded as essential to sustained success. It confirms the shift from the more traditional focus on the intelligence quotient (IQ) to a better balance with the emotional intelligence quotient (EQ). In a recent article in *Harvard Business Review* on succession, Richard Haythornthwaite and Ajay Banga, respectively the former chair and current chair of Mastercard, wrote that "the financial market company now talks a lot not just about IQ and EQ (emotional intelligence) but also about DQ ('decency quotient')."[1] I have sometimes spoken of RIQ as a factor to watch for in leaders: the "righteous indignation quotient." It is all about self-awareness, gaining feedback, and then the willingness to adjust. We do see research starting to point to self-awareness in driving leader success. The softer skills are always the blind spots on which leaders need to focus as they renew their own beliefs and actions.

Empathy Is Out of the Shadows

What we are discussing here is empathy in leading. This means awareness of the essential role played by those around you in helping you lead. There is no contradiction between showing empathy and being decisive and single-minded in pursuit of objectives and goals. Mary Jo Haddad is clear on this:

> When we say "people matter," this is empty if you're not taking into account the impact of your decisions on people. Or, to put it another way, if you lack empathy. The imperious and impervious style has failed time and time again. Those who are very top-down and directive often are at a loss to understand why the style is not working. No question is ever asked about how we could do this better; no connection is made between making impactful decisions and mitigating the risk on the people around you who are actually carrying out the work to support your vision. Empathy does not mean backing off or quitting. If there's something you want, go for it – and recognize that lots of people are around to enable you to get there. Single-mindedness is a strength. It

can be learned, especially if you realize that focus and defiance does not mean "I did it my way" alone, without the help of others.

Mary Jo identifies why we have seen the concept of empathy resisted and considered soft and not suitable in a business context. While this attitude is changing, it still conjures beliefs that being empathetic means having to cater to everyone's needs lest one be judged to be tough and uncaring. But, as EQ is better understood and given attention, this false belief is waning. We now better understand that empathy is rising very high on the list of the requirements most valued today in leaders.

The experience of the COVID-19 pandemic has certainly pushed the importance of leaders having both empathy and compassion, in being able to walk in others' shoes, understand their perspectives, and respond to the greater good. They must exercise this in the context of the other person's needs and the organization's needs. Leaders will not survive without it. Such softer skills are not a paradox nor a competing priority but a clear obligation of leaders to lead in today's realities.

Personal Values Now Get More Attention

What leaders stand for now gets more attention than ever: the trust they earn from all stakeholders, including customers and employees, is under scrutiny. A leader's motivations for intentions and behavior are often seen to stem from personal values – a code that drives our actions. Personal values are often wondered about when *empathy* is absent as well as when one's *character* is questioned. This is especially so as our mindset and beliefs more influentially guide our humanity and affect others.

intended more often for junior-to-mid-level employees and more seldom for senior-level leaders. This chapter illuminates another belief and myth that exists about mentoring and applies, to some degree, more broadly to the mindset held by many that formal mentoring is also less required by accomplished leaders. This mindset stems from the line of thinking that formal education is both sufficient and sustainable for leadership competencies. Yet it is worthwhile to consider opinions on this topic of overreliance on formalized education, including opinions from business schools.

When asked for advice by a CEO or other leader, one of my first questions is: "Do you have a mentor or a confidant/sounding board?" Every leader gets this question from me. They also get my second comment, which is: "Please consider this right away." Even leaders attending my class at the Rotman School of Management are asked this question before we begin the class discussion. The conversation often shifts to an exchange about the belief that mentoring is for "others" or only if you have a problem or mainly for beginners. All of this is true; and it is encouraging that leaders do recognize the value of mentoring, which is increasingly evident in talent considerations. As much as 20 per cent of formal development now accounts for mentoring, up from 5 per cent, whereas 70 per cent accounts for other job assignments and 10 per cent for classroom courses and so forth – a good ratio.

As students of leadership, though, it is a shame that mentoring, as a source of and a boost for a leader's learning throughout their journey, is missing. It is an unfortunate loss when leaders falsely assume that they are too senior or too advanced or too smart or formally educated to need, or benefit from, a mentor. I do encounter this mindset in some situations. Luckily, research is showing that up to 80 per cent of CEOs in many surveys say they do engage with one or even two mentors in some form. It can be a mentoring-type relationship with a wise sounding board, a friend, or other more general adviser. They might not even refer to it as mentoring or acknowledge it explicitly.

Some Have Several Mentors!

Marc-André Blanchard, as well as most of the accomplished leaders sharing stories in this book, comments on this topic of mentors: "Oh yes, I have had a long list of mentors whom I regularly call for advice. Many have been a source of 'go to' for over a decade. It is core to my success." While Marc-André was in school, he looked for role models, people he could look up to. He learned how to engage and make relationships. The concept of help from others, he says, began with his parents and the parents of friends from school. This set the foundation for connecting and looking for opportunities to learn from others whom he considered role models. Now he focuses on younger people whom he mentors – but they also mentor him. Marc-André typifies the progressive type of mentoring that is now emerging, known as "reverse mentoring." He learned it from his Canadian Mission team at the United Nations, which was filled with younger people and from whom he learned so much.[1]

Ron Farmer speaks similarly about the importance of mentorship during his time at McKinsey, where they use a core model of mentorship for the ongoing development of leaders. Leaders were actually evaluated on the extent to which they themselves mentored others and received mentoring. Mentorship to Ron is a natural part of leading. He sees that being both a mentor and mentee is the obligation of all leaders.

Uncover Blind Spots

A mentor generally helps to uncover a leader's blind spot or a hidden strength. Increasingly, we see testimony and endorsement from CEOs and others who cite the significant benefits they receive from mentors. Such benefits can include enhanced decision-making and improved performance outcomes. They can also include avoiding costly mistakes by rethinking a strategy or plan. Those are powerful endorsements that debunk the myth of mentoring as being best for "others." For the many who do not engage in mentors or in any meaningful way seek other intentional and deliberate learning moments, there are many underlying reasons why this exists, often fueled by the belief that it is "others" who require improvement.

Why Are Mentors Resisted?

Unfortunately, despite progress, this latter belief persists, not unlike other long-held beliefs that give us false confidence. It can also stem from many other causes, including a previous experience. In my experience, there are four common themes that can make leaders blind to the value of mentoring, which are described as follows.

Perception of Weakness?
The fact that leaders sometimes fear that having a mentor will create a perception of having a weakness and not being up to the job. This brings to mind the (false) belief that being a good leader means having all the answers. This habit of not seeking help is not uncommon.

Low on Humility?
The reality that some leaders are lacking in humility or self-awareness is a typical blind spot that leads to the belief of self-sufficiency. Those leaders often have a solid track record, not many failures, and are locked

into the belief that their leadership is timeless. Such a shame.

Bad Previous Experience?
Among the leaders with whom I have worked closely, I have met many who've had a previous bad experience. This is often the case of poor choice of mentor or that the advice received was suboptimal. This is a common flaw and reflects the fact that just as there are leaders who have deficiencies, so too there are mentors. The choice of a mentor is very important and is further reviewed in chapter 22.

Righteous Indignation?
Situations exist where there is a touch of righteous indignation or egotistical tendencies that stand in the way. Happily, we now see less of those mindsets about mentoring.

Checking your thoughts about getting a mentor or even a second mentor is one of the best things every leader can do. And you can start right now, today! It can be a huge breakthrough in your career journey or help tremendously in overcoming a hurdle with which you are struggling. What is the worst thing that can happen? You might learn something that "just confirms what you know" – and that, too, is reassuring!

In addition to the compelling stories about the critical importance of mentoring for accomplished leaders (and lower-level leaders), it is equally compelling to consider the current demands that did not exist for leaders even a few years ago. It is not uncommon to lead with the mindset that, once we become a good leader and are recognized as such, we are okay. There is a danger of becoming comfortable and even oblivious to the changing context and its implication for leading differently.

Leaders Are Expected to Raise Their Game

However, the reality is that leaders are now expected to raise their game. Their thinking is being challenged more often; they have to make decisions that they have never tackled before. They are expected to react to and solve a new crisis. And their obligations to boards have increased; boards and all governing bodies today are forceful and powerful and have increasingly divergent views to be heard and respected.

As one of my leader colleagues expressed it – and is echoed in different ways by others – it gets lonely at the top! It is not unusual to have recurring self-doubts and have to cope with significant stress. This happens to many leaders because they were never prepared for what has come and continues to come their way. Once one becomes a leader, the pathway to the top narrows, and the available and approachable options also narrow. This is all different and naturally many leaders struggle with the change. Mentoring helps. Self-renewal becomes a standard!

Everyone needs a mentor!

CHAPTER NINE

High Performers Do Not Always Equal High Potential for Leadership

> Our leadership pipelines are often inadequate, and our discovery of this inadequacy is always too late.
>
> **Rose M. Patten**

There are many reasons why we have this reality, many of which are correlated with the premises of this book – such as leadership is dynamic; leadership is hard; leadership constantly needs renewal of key elements; leadership is *not* timeless. However, there are other key factors related to our beliefs about "who and what" make the best choice and best source of good leaders, based on the most highly valued capabilities for leading in these extraordinary times.

Leadership Growth

How does good leadership form and grow? It is now known that high performers are not always high leadership potential. However, the beliefs of many leaders are not aligned with this truth; their actions and habits demonstrate this. Only in more recent years have we begun to more systematically distinguish and discern what would constitute high potential for taking on leadership roles – and how to identify them for "the pool" feeding into the leadership pipeline.

It is generally accepted that one of the greatest obligations of leaders is "picking and developing other leaders." It is not just about picking followers, although that, too, is a long-standing belief. Yet all too often replacement candidates are in short supply or a possible candidate is not ready; or there is only one to choose from when making the final decision. Naturally, many leaders do pride themselves on the ability to spot talent and bring it along. But as organizational challenges and leading become more complex, leaders are finding out they need to do much better. Relying on former assumptions about choosing leaders can be suboptimal. Challenges related to succession when openings occur or to the shortage of supply in leadership pipelines and lack of readiness are strong indicators of this reality (as referenced in chapter 1, supported by studies and opinions).

Choosing the Wrong Leader – Stranded Costs!

There is much research on the cost and impact arising from poor placement of talent in significant roles (and not just from poor senior leader replacements). Darryl White speaks to the consequences of putting the wrong person in a position or giving them the wrong mandate. "Even if you go back and try to fix it, there are so many stranded costs. The person being replaced would already have had far reaching impacts on many others. Making people mistakes places you in a big dilemma. Correcting the mistake quickly may look like the issue is resolved but it lingers for a long time." As Darryl puts it, this is where we have to think about how talent meets strategy. It's important that we always remember just what the problems are that we want the particular leader and teams to solve. "In other words, recruitment and the promotion of leaders have to be forward-leading. It cannot be like saying: 'Oh, there's a high performer, so let's just put him/her into the pool or the position at hand.' Instead, the question should be: 'What capabilities truly drive high performance – are they the ones needed in the future?' High performance is not always moveable or 'plug and play.' What people were good at in their current role may not be what is needed for the next role going forward." Darryl is clearly making the point that has been proven in so many talent management decisions: high performance is *situational* and cannot be assumed to be the same as high potential for a given role such as leadership.

Spotting Potential

My own revelation on discovering flaws in spotting and identifying high potentials for leadership was troublesome. It was a setback from what I thought was being achieved. This happened when I was chief human resources officer at BMO Financial Group. BMO had a deserved reputation for advanced talent management practices, especially those related to developing talent and high-potential pools. My story confirms that high performance does not automatically equal high potential for leadership. The assumption widely held at the time was that we should set the goal of having 10 per cent of a given population identified as high potential. My talent team and I were able to achieve this and proudly believed that we were enriching and boosting the organization's talent pipelines. Every leader in every division was engaged in identifying their high-potential employees (HIPOs). The number we collectively reached was 500.

Flawed Assessment

However, the setback came when we had openings in vice-president positions and the head of talent came to me and said, "We do not have a clear candidate ready to fill this role at this time." How could this be? With such a pool, there should have been several with the leadership potential to be promoted. Just as Darryl points out, there was a big disconnect in what the new role needed versus the capabilities of those identified as high potential. The question was whether it was (a) poor assessment in putting them in the pool in the first place; (b) inadequate development in their leadership training; or (c) too much bias by the manager doing the identification. We went to find out. The outcome of our analysis was, first, after recalibration of the 500 HIPOs, the number became 350. We learned that the cause of this inflation to 500 was related to several factors. One factor was poorly defined requirements for what constituted leadership potential in today's environment. A second factor was far too much emphasis on in-the-moment high performance. A third was the halo effect coming from assessors having selected candidates in their own image.

Potential for What?

This was a wake-up call. It propelled me on a path of exploration and specificity on the criteria to be used for identifying and confirming leader potential with reasonable certainty. The term "high potential," while generously used, was not consistently defined and therefore not fully reliable in its outcomes. It begged the question of "high potential" for what? For what now constitutes the effective leader had changed and needed to be understood and considered by those in the selection process. Today, much progress has been made and significant strategies for leader development formalized and mandated. The responsibility for identifying and nurturing high potential is hard and often underestimated. In subsequent years, since that big learning experience, I have made three distinct and relevant discoveries about developing leaders. I now apply and advise other leaders of those discoveries, which are worthy of passing on here.

Finding Number One
High potential is situational! Just as high performance is situational, high potential can increase or decrease with time and, of course, with the changes in leadership requirements resulting from the changing context. This should not be surprising. It is akin to the reality that leadership is not timeless. The notion that "once a great leader, always a great leader" is flawed. The sad thing about assumed "high potentials" can be that they don't always get a chance to be effective (or ineffective) because they do not, or should not, make it into the pool to begin with – as research shows.

Finding Number Two
High performers are not always automatically high potential. To believe that they are is, unfortunately, a natural and long-held assumption by leaders when they identify high potential candidates. This was a partial cause in the BMO case and in many other cases. It again reflects the point that Darryl made. The tendency is to pick the highest performing or the smartest employee because they are more like the assessor – also known as picking in your image. Some startling facts from research by CCL (Center for Creative Leadership) confirm this reality. In

the pools examined by CCL, there were three consistent outcomes:

30 per cent truly have the potential to rise	40 per cent do not belong in the pool of emerging leaders	30 per cent are borderline but can make it

Finding Number Three
Knowing who the true high potentials are versus those who are not high potential is significant. Truly high potentials are seen to be twice as valuable and three times as likely to succeed as future leaders.

Leader Behaviors: Often Missed

It has been observed that the capabilities most often lacking in potential leaders identified for talent pools fall into the following categories: motivating others, relating to others (empathy), delegating to others, and inspiring others. These are essential requirements for today's leadership effectiveness. By contrast, the capabilities more typically identified are technical skills, capacity for learning, and initiative. This reminds us that yesterday's assumptions about what is important in leadership need to be renewed. Old beliefs need debunking. What we are learning is that the biggest oversight or weakness in identifying leadership potential and managing talent for building leadership pipelines is, unsurprisingly, that specific leader behaviors and requirements are not properly codified or set out. This is another example of past beliefs impeding success.

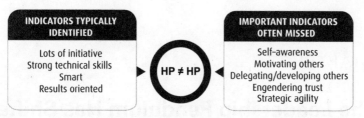

FIGURE 11. High Performance Does Not Equal High Potential

The primary intention of this chapter has been to debunk the long-held beliefs that (a) higher performers equal high potential and (b) leaders always come from a high-performing pool. Both assumptions are flawed without a careful reflection on what leaders are required to do within the current context, conditions, and challenges. This represents one more instance in which leaders need to check their current beliefs and practices about the best paths to becoming a leader for today's culture and requirements.

The Big 8 will help address this, as readers reflect on their own mindsets and, more importantly, on how leadership is evolving and on which capabilities are most highly valued today.

CHAPTER TEN

The Leadership Pendulum Has Shifted

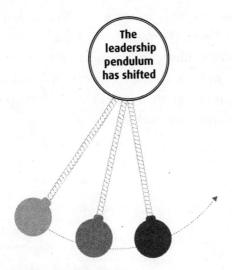

FIGURE 12. The Leadership Pendulum

Questions Continue

Part 1 discussed why leadership is changing and why it is harder. We saw that this is related to those "defining moments" experienced by many in their leadership careers, as well as to expectations of leading better in these extraordinary times of ever-increasing disruption. From this analysis we identified three external unmistakable game changers as being causes of why leadership is changing and why it's harder.

Part 2 then discussed barriers that stand in the way of mastering the unmistakable game changers and leading well in times of disruption and change. Such barriers are related to internal conditions and are strongly influenced by the leader's mindset, long-held beliefs, and perpetual habits. These result in false confidence and static practices contribute to less-effective leading.

Is Leadership Shifting?

At this point, there are two bigger questions that need our attention. What do leaders have to do differently, or more or less of, or not at all? What is, or will be, more valued and sought from across all sectors? In other words, is leadership shifting? To answer this, we have to realize that nothing stands still. As we saw earlier in chapter 6, leadership is *not timeless*. It does not stay the same, nor does it stop and start. I liken it to a *pendulum*, shifting and settling in a different place as conditions change. That's what a leader is – a continuum of past, present, and still-evolving practices, influenced by the internal and external conditions of the times in which we live. But also influenced by the leader's own mindset, beliefs, and worthiness.

No Lasting Formula

There is no lasting formula for the perfect way to lead: no straight line, no injections of any one thing. It's just ongoing learning and adjusting and self-renewal. This means that leading must be *intentional* – going beyond pure instinct or acting on yesterday's assumptions. It entails much more reflection, more listening, more observation, and a more open mind – all of which are powered by the leader's degree of adaptability. This book is based on the rise in emphasis on the human side of leading. Leading better begins and ends with the human dynamic at the center. Specific capabilities are therefore required to focus on this human dynamic. But mastery of such capabilities will not happen unless leaders are *intentional* about adopting and practicing them.

Leadership comes from many roots and in many forms. Yes, there are many people whose position and role are categorically that of leading formally. However, the simple truth is that leading happens whenever people find themselves, or choose to be, involved in actions and responsibilities that connect with others and impact them. The goal of leading well is that the positive impact on others' energy produces better outcomes. Such examples include:

- Helping a person make sense of a situation, offering greater clarification and helpful perspectives;
- Encouraging others to imagine different ways to solve a problem;
- Inspiring others to join in and move toward achieving an accomplishment;
- Building trust and growth in others and showing empathy;
- Encouraging fortitude for sticking with hard-to-do acts;
- Acting as a personal role model.

Considering that most of humanity is in some way on this journey (not just those with titles or big incomes), there is some form of leadership around everyone. Judging from the hundreds of personal stories I've listened to, I firmly believe that leadership is within the purview of many and most. Better leadership, therefore, is the standard sought after, and hoped for, by all. It is not just for a select few or for those who are emerging as leaders.

Leading with Intention Enables the Shift

Given that we are in a pendulum shift, the successful leader will have to know what to stop doing and what to do more of or differently. This is the essence of leading with *intention* and deliberate habits. As Aristotle said: "Excellence is not a mere action, but a habit! What we choose to do repeatedly."

Intentionality means a shift *from* a non-reflective and instinctive action *to* pausing and reflecting on the important things to be accomplished and the different ways to engage others. We are reminded of Darryl White's *intentional map*, which he has deliberately embraced and constantly applied in leading differently. Indeed, he believes he would have failed without it. Leaders can derail without this intention. Instinct is not enough! Shifting *from* instinctive actions, often driven by a command or directive-like approach, *to* a more open and intentional approach is echoed by Tiff Macklem in our conversation about handling a crisis. "Leaders have to be prepared to react to unanticipated crisis and risks. They can arise from many quarters, propelled by a range of human and technical factors. Reacting to a crisis, in today's leading, is a worthy experience; it develops a whole new 'set of muscles' to meet and subdue the problem. Investing in contingency planning is vital. Still, when the crisis does hit, it won't be what you planned for. You will need an open mind, a readiness to jettison memory muscles and old patterns of the past."

The pendulum shift of being intentional and less instinctive is also preceded by a wake-up call – namely, discovering that leaders are *not* expected to have all the answers! A long-held – but mistaken – belief is that, once you are appointed a leader, you are expected to have all the answers. There are many downsides to this belief and way of leading – as I have discovered. Leaders can exhaust themselves from this belief about having all the answers; they also impede the growth and learning of others. In addition, they encounter the discontent and frustration of others in the expectations of our workforces, whose mindset means more involvement, more consultation, and more empowerment.

Distributed Leadership

As a leader, I went *from* this mindset of having to have all the answers *to* the practice of distributed leadership (as it is now commonly known). In other words, I went to leading through more inclusion, more collaboration, more consultation – and therefore through enabling others. Much credit for my renewed thinking goes to my time as chair of the governing council at the University of Toronto. The norm there is serious and wide consultation, gaining inputs on all important decisions. From this experience came not only much invigoration but also the realization of the power of having "multiple inputs." Having such inputs is the gold standard for decision-making – in particular, as we shall see, for decisions related to the selection of leaders.

> **Inclusion, collaboration, and consultation is the path to distributed leadership.**

Communication Is Vital

Mary Jo Haddad is filled with insights and personal stories about the pendulum shift in the approach to decision-making and the engagement of others. "Communication is vital. It is the means through which you show transparency – not just on the what of one's decisions, but more importantly the why." That is the reason she goes so deeply and energetically into communications, well beyond the goals and objectives of the organization. It started when she noticed more and more people showing up for her briefings when she was CEO. She is certain it was attributable to the fact that she explained *why* the organization's leadership chose to do certain things. "There is a ripple effect – when the CEO is out on the 'shop floor' and is accessible and inclusive in communicating and explaining the why; then the next levels of leaders start doing the same. This is showing how you lead and appeals to the head and heart. People respect this."

It Adds Up to Connecting Well with Others

Moving from command and control to connect and collaborate is powered by the multiple ways in which leaders can and do connect vertically and horizontally with and without hierarchy, depending on the situation. The concept of connecting has now become plentiful and situational. In his book *The Tipping Point*, Malcolm Gladwell describes connectors "as someone with an extraordinary knack of making friends and acquaintances."[1] This brilliant insight has become widely spread and its evolution now incorporates the power of connection and its positive impact well beyond friendships and charisma. Its inclusion in leading better and in harnessing the discretionary energy of others is widely recognized and increasingly resonating. Enlightening examples of connectivity and its power can be found in "10 Life-Changing Tips from Top Connectors" by Sally Horchow.[2] This is one of many examples of how connectivity can empower leaders to connect effectively and to bring out the best in oneself and others.

Character Continues to Matter More

We also see the pendulum shifting position on who and what leaders are expected to be and what they stand for. In a word: their character. The spotlight is on character like never before, eclipsing experience, expertise, even a past success record. Character has become more topical and less silent, particularly in the aftermath of the financial crisis from a decade ago. The heightened increase in stakeholder expectations means that character is no longer assumed, no matter what a leader's overall credentials may be. Instead, it is a prominent factor in a leader's worthiness and survival.

Janice Gross Stein describes character and trustworthiness, whether in crisis or normal times: "Character is not always intact nor immutable, it can develop more explicitly out of crisis. Character, trust, and integrity have many dimensions. But without it, a leader cannot succeed." Moreover, character and integrity are revealed during crisis. "The global financial meltdown of over a decade ago and today's COVID-19 pandemic are the bookends of two real crises. One of the biggest tests of leadership is coming up with actions while knowing that the success of those actions will not be known until later. Does a crisis really change leadership? There is some evidence that it does. For example, from the global financial crisis came the recognition that character and treating people properly really matter." Her point speaks to the swing from silence about to an explicit emphasis on character in what is expected of leadership. Assuming it is no longer enough.

The Big 8 Crystallizes

The pendulum depicted below shows the shift *from* what has been traditionally valued and accepted in leaders *to* what is now expected and emphasized. It illuminates how and why intentional leadership not only matters but is necessary. It raises the question of *what capabilities* are now required to master this pendulum shift in leading. The Big 8 capabilities answer that question by making sense of the pendulum shift; they explain more tangibly the essence of leading better, not just for today but also for tomorrow in our transforming world.

Part 1 concludes with describing the unmistakable game changers – increased stakeholder expectations; dramatically changing workforces and workplaces; and the dominance of short-lived strategies and digitalization. Part 2 concludes with combining these with long-held beliefs and myths – a leader's way of thinking, believing, acting, and impacting others. *Together, parts 1 and 2 are driving the pendulum shift and recognizing the Big 8 capabilities.* These are the new realities for leaders to consider and adapt to, as they demonstrate their worthiness of having the great privilege of being a leader. How they adapt is what will set leaders apart. They will need to be intentional in their leadership with newly defined capabilities. It is now that we move to what these capabilities are – the Big 8.

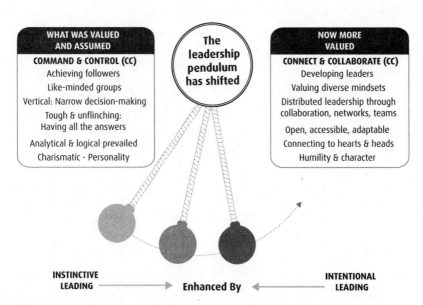

FIGURE 13. The Leadership Pendulum Has Shifted

PART THREE

The Big 8 Crystallizes – Setting Leaders Apart

CHAPTER ELEVEN

Where and How the Big 8 Fit in a Leader's Overall Role

The exploration and discovery of how the Big 8 would fit within a leader's role has been discussed, debated, and agreed through twenty-five sessions, each lasting one week, in the Rotman School of Management and the BMO Executive Leadership Programs from 2010 onwards. Each of the eight defining capabilities was used as a case study in class and many nuances were confirmed. Each capability held strong throughout detailed analysis and testing, providing compelling proof of its effectiveness in leading better, with emphasis on the human dimensions, as always.

From "Command and Control" to "Connect and Collaborate"

As shown in the pendulum shift discussion (chapter 10), the Big 8 defining capabilities recognize that the human dynamics of connecting and collaborating move leaders *away from* the traditional tendency to lead via command and control *to* connect and collaborate. This

The human side of leading is rising.

way of leading is far more multifaceted. Harnessing discretionary energy – while sharing power and at the same time gaining trust – demands understanding the nuances of connecting well with others. It takes multiple capabilities such as those codified in the Big 8. It will not happen without them. This is certain.

Different forms of communication; more personal presence with teams; greater ability to relate and inspire without the power of one's position but rather through the personal power of inspiration and personal leadership – all such contrasts were depicted in the pendulum shift in chapter 10. Leaders are dependent upon, and guided by, their own individual level of self-awareness, gained from self-reflection and feedback from others. This enables them to take deliberate, intentional action to check and adjust their mindset. No one else can be responsible.

So, it is not new that this human side of leading has been growing in demand and setting leaders apart. Such capabilities were readily self-identified by the leaders who tell their stories through this book as well as the many others involved in the teaching, advising, and study described in it. All of them have engaged in self-renewal in multiple ways. Self-renewal and the obligation of developing others are now seen as table stakes for leading well. Reflection and self-awareness are the critical underpinnings of this action. At the core of being a worthwhile leader is caring about your impact on others and the determination that such impact be positive. Having positive impact relies on a mindset focused on, and a commitment to, empathy, personal values, and character and trust. These are what enable a leader to communicate with a route to the heart as well as to the head. They come from intentional leadership and lead inevitably to greater success. Together with other Big 8 capabilities, they add a "connect and collaborate" way of leading, which is one of the most challenging adjustments for even successful leaders to make.

The Big 8

A decade of study, observation, and practices – plus hands-on engagement with widely spread and diverse leaders – stands behind the Big 8 and the concept of leading with intention. Now, in the following chapters, the Big 8 is explained in terms of *why* each capability responds to both the unmistakable game changers and the long-held beliefs, myths, and habits; *why* each meets the criteria to be one of the select eight; and *how* each one reflects the nuances needed for leaders to think differently about past assumptions. Even when one of the capabilities might be familiar, it is nonetheless important to reflect on it for a moment. A caution is appropriate here: the Big 8 is *not* a panacea. It does not address all the skills that leaders are expected to have. Rather, the Big 8 offers the solution for leaders to become more effective and better balanced in their leading.

The overall performance dimensions of a leader in getting the job done with good results rely on the requisite technical, strategic, and financial expertise. These have received consistent attention over the years from business schools as well as in-house corporate training programs. Many of the Big 8 capabilities could be seen as softer skills by some. They are looked for in today's leaders. The Big 8 also recognize the more horizontal perspectives essential for leaders, which are often absent or underutilized in a more silo-oriented, vertical mindset. For leaders to lead horizontally across boundaries (and thereby not have full control and authority over all related activities), they will have to rely on their own fine-tuned people skills and the ever-more complex human dynamics of the changing workforce.

Leading Vertically and Horizontally

Increasing recognition of broader, more balanced leadership capabilities first showed up in the 1990s in a concept called "T" leadership, designed to fill the gap brought about by the need to lead across boundaries. This "T" leadership concept attempted to address the horizontal and broader cross-unit nature of leveraging the entire organization's strengths. Leading by influence, increased collaboration, inclusiveness across groups and teams – these all began to take shape. They included different forms of communication; more connection with people; and greater ability to relate and inspire – often without the power of the position but connecting with others through "personal" power and personal leadership. The spotlight moved to more inclusive leadership, which in turn highlighted a big rise in human skills (or softer skills), in addition to the more technical, financial, strategic, and technological expertise required for effective leading.

Even though such human skills have been rising in demand for some time, their acceptance by leaders has moved more slowly. However, chapter 7 debunked the belief that such "softer" skills would improve with time. The Big 8 selects the exact capabilities for achieving human skills and this more effective and balanced leadership. Every leader will need to incorporate – and very intentionally practice – this greater emphasis on the Big 8 as a means to being a better leader.

In the following chapters, I will describe the nuances of the Big 8 capabilities individually and collectively. Each of the Big 8 capabilities will stand alone as separate actions to be intensified as called for. Many are overlapping, intertwined, and can be combined. This explains the "why" these eight were selected and grouped as representing the most critical human skills in today's extraordinary times.

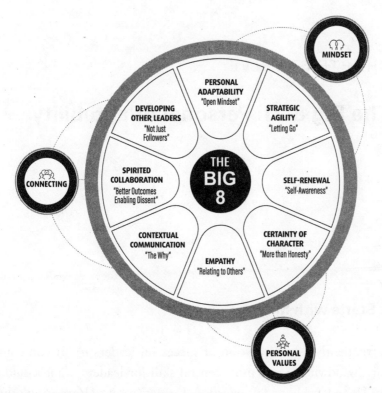

FIGURE 14. The Big 8 and Its Three Clusters

The Big 8 form into three clusters as a way to frame those capabilities that are likely companions and those that draw on a leader's core essence of leading in the most human-centric manner.

CHAPTER TWELVE

The Big 8 #1: Personal Adaptability

It Starts with Mindset

A frequently asked question of successful leaders is: "If you could narrow down the one most central skill for leaders, what would it be?" It's a hard but a fair question. Leaders want to learn from other leaders and every leader should be able to prioritize the one, two, or even three most critical skills within their own context. I now ask this of many leaders, and I always get asked that question myself.

What Is Your Answer?

The views of other leaders are found in their stories throughout parts 1 and 2 of this book, with more to come in ensuing chapters. Personal adaptability is very explicitly mentioned by each leader interviewed. My answer to this question has been the same for decades: personal adaptability. I name this as a central reason for my own success. It is the first skill I intentionally watch for in my interactions with others, in whatever capacity situations arise. What is my stance? Do I have an open mind? Am I adaptable?

Adaptability was for me a bit easier than some other capabilities in the Big 8. It was certainly necessary in my career journey from very early on, due to the different sectors I led; the diverse cultures represented in these sectors; and the geographies – locally, nationally, internationally – where they were located. I strongly believe that I would not have had such a diverse and successful leadership journey had I not developed and continuously refined this capability of personal adaptability. Whether in the varied sectors of banking, academia, health, public policy, the arts – all were C-suite roles involving complex leading. It was hard to adapt in each, but necessary. Being adaptable is very intentional – instinct alone is not enough.

Checking One's Stance

Tiff Macklem speaks of the technique of "always checking one's stance" – counting on a whole new set of muscles to meet the challenge in front of you. "In handling any crisis or new situation, solutions are not written down, they don't come from a quote book; they inherently have lots of potential risk. But you can't be paralyzed or rely on old assumptions that worked before. Yes, you can be informed by them; but being open and adaptable enables you to react to the unanticipated, the unfamiliar."

Mindset Matters

To begin or continue striving to be more adaptable, start with a pre-check of mindset. As a leader, you own your mindset and beliefs – and therefore the outcomes of your actions and decisions. It's best not to wait until the situation confronts you. The time to pre-check is now. Every leader can be intentional and deliberate and not leave actions to pure instinct or taken in the moment. In conversation with Mary Jo Haddad, she speaks of personal adaptability and organizational agility as critical for a CEO to master. "It comes from seeing opportunity in a crisis, staying grounded on what is essential, adapting as the situation warrants. When you are leading a large public organization like a hospital, you don't have control over demand for service, nor are there resources to support innovations for the future. Leaders must be adaptable, creative, open-minded."

For Mary Anne Chambers, adaptability, open-mindedness, and renewal are overlapping, one leading to another. Open-mindedness enables adaptability to occur; with adaptability, the hope of renewal is possible. She speaks of "the premium" she placed on her own personal adaptability as she worked across sectors, always making sure she opened her mindset to understand and adapt to the differences and nuances in policies, culture, and thinking of others. When asked where this kind of adaptability comes from, Mary Anne replies: "It comes from being a lifelong learner, especially on issues related to people and injustice. I'm the daughter of Jamaican parents, growing up in a traditional family. The way I look at life and at others has been inspired by a deep curiosity about people – it's part of my nature, which my parents were able to support in many ways. My mother, though very wise, lacked formal education. I realized from an early age that education would be key to my future." When asked why she, then a mother of young sons and working at Scotiabank, was taking university night courses, she answers: "I didn't want not having a degree to be a barrier to my career. Possibilities could arise in my work, and I wanted to be formally equipped to take advantage of them."

What It Takes to Be More Adaptable

We come to the central question of whether the individual leader can embrace new or different dimensions of a problem. Can the person tackle unfamiliar territory with an open mind? Can one listen, learn, add value and, even if not in agreement, remain open? Personal adaptability takes several beliefs, habits, and intentions.

None of this is easily done. Leadership is hard. But such are the demands on the leader. This is what it takes to be adaptable and to sustain it. They are the elements of leading well and are now preoccupying leaders who reflect on being better.

Discussion with senior leaders in the classroom and other testing of the important ingredients for adaptability raised other points of debate. A point of concern is *how one reconciles adaptability with authenticity.* The debate focused on the belief that adaptability and authenticity go hand in hand. Leaders are expected to do both. Authenticity is not a static, unwavering identity, nor is it an excuse for sticking to what's most comfortable. Better

Strong and unflinching leaders can adapt.

leaders combine the two, which leads to earning trust. Being authentic cannot survive without an open mind. Nor can an open mind blossom without authenticity. Better leaders view adaptability as a true form of continuous learning and a means to embrace change.

A second frequent point of concern focuses on the difficulty in shifting *from* the previously valued and familiar "strong and unflinching leader" *to* the adaptive and open leader who knows they don't know it all and is open to the possibility of being wrong or at least acknowledges having insufficient knowledge or know-how. Humility – and the lack of it – allows us to see how easy it is for leaders to lose perspective when they become senior and hold positions of power and success, falling into the trap of believing one is invincible, invaluable, even infallible. So, what is the incentive for the hard work of adapting? The incentive is leading well, having positive impact, being worthy of the privilege of leading, and avoiding irrelevance or failure.

A third point of concern relates to setbacks and stumbles that occur frequently when leaders make changes. This is not just about pride and embarrassments; it is about the increased stress, now more pervasive than ever, in coping with relentless demands while being time-starved and increasingly multitasked. This is now recognized as EADS (executive attention deficit disorder syndrome). Methods for developing resilience to EADS were discussed in the classroom, with a separate, highly recommended body of knowledge emerging. It comes back to the expected role of the leader and the mental toughness a leader needs in order to endure, succeed, and be distinctive. As we will see, it's about courage and fortitude to change.[1]

What It Takes to Be More Adaptable

Requirements	Actions – Behaviors
❖ Open vs. closed mindset	❖ Accepting diverse views
❖ Embracing disruption	❖ Let go of being comfortable
❖ Tackling unfamiliar territory	❖ Energy, optimism, mental toughness
❖ Handling setbacks	❖ Strong resilient actions
❖ Responding to relentless demands	

BEING RESILIENT

CHAPTER THIRTEEN

The Big 8 #2: Strategic Agility

It Starts with Mindset

The Big 8 calls for an open mind to enable leaders to become more agile in seizing strategic opportunities. It means letting go of the comfortable and familiar tenets of past strategic scenarios. For some, this can be even more difficult than personally adapting to day-to-day challenges. And so much more seems at stake these days with greater risk and uncertainty at play.

Strategies Are Short-Lived

The rise of digitalization has made strategic agility one of the unmistakable game changers for leaders. Agility for strategic success is consequently far more visible and inescapable. Everyone can see its absence in a company whose status is frail and whose strategies are outdated. No leader is exempt. Strategies are short-lived, while new and innovative ones are hard to get going, even for those quick to recognize this and act. Companies that ponder too long due to low agility on the part of their decision-makers are outrun pretty quickly. This unpredictability is at the root of the struggles that many leaders are now having.

In conversation and through other forms of input for this book, leaders raise, without prompting, the importance of strategic agility. Darryl White is one. He places a high premium both on individual personal adaptability and on agility in leading strategically. He describes how the leader's role has evolved during his own career journey:

> Leadership is about navigating turbulence and confronting it head-on. Over my 30-year career, with the last two decades in a leadership position, crisis and turbulence have been a constant. The leadership period started with 9/11; then came the fracturing of the global financial system over three years from 2007 to 2009. Now it's the COVID-19 pandemic. Compare that to the fifty-five-year period after the end of World War II. Crises were relatively light. With the main financial and social structures generally in place, it was an era of prosperity and a more predictable time. This was the earlier generation's model for setting the direction of an organization and in managing people. However, for the past twenty years, leaders haven't had that "luxury." Today, the premium is instead on agility, on building in a better understanding of what the risks are, where they can be found, and what happens if they materialize. Risk models in the banking industry didn't exist twenty-five years ago. Such models have emerged since, almost simultaneously with the advancement of digital technology, and are imperative for today's leaders who operate in the constant presence of disruption and change.

Personal Adaptability Enhances Strategic Agility

A common question is whether a leader who has adapted well personally and exercises an open mind to individual problems day to day can also readily be strategically agile. Like all of the Big 8, these two important capabilities – adaptability and strategic agility – are easily combined and are mutually enhancing, not duplicative or exclusive to one another as either/or. Both call for the underpinning of having an open mind. And leaders need both. Each has different challenges at stake. The magnitude of navigating disruption and making fast, sound, competitive strategic choices requires a breadth of agility, critical thinking, and far-reaching perspectives that go beyond the personal adaptability required to embrace differences in a more vertical or narrow situation.

My conversation with Meric Gertler reveals how strategic agility was harnessed by his teams during the COVID-19 pandemic but was enabled by personal adaptability skills:

If there's any silver lining to COVID-19, it is the importance of adaptability. Being compelled to adapt by the pandemic has provided experience that will pay dividends. We had to answer in real time – can we cope? Are we agile and flexible? Do we have the necessary dedication, the commitment and creativity, to adapt, survive – and be successful? The answer is yes. We now have proof positive.

Agility and adaptability are needed in other areas of university life. Global engagement, for example. How do our students have a global experience? How do we connect our research internationally? We've learned that you can't do things as you once did. Now everything must be done more remotely. Accordingly, we've created the "global classroom" to team up with others in teaching classes together and having students work collaboratively across borders.

This has been an eye-opener. The template for this kind of engagement was developed before COVID-19 but hadn't been tested. Today we have proposals for seventy-five of these setups across the university and people are embracing them. The same is true with our research partnerships. Contrary to expectations, this kind of engagement is going up, not down, with new partnerships and new people. There are questions, of course. Are people trusting these new forms of interaction? Can you build a long-lasting relationship through such modalities? Not sure, but it means we're a more agile institution going forward.

Dynamic vs. Static: Market-Based vs. Proprietary

Strategies and digitalization are now all about being dynamic. Any notion of a static mindset will perish. Such stories testify that strategy has become more dependent on vision, market knowledge, and critical thinking, combined with a mindset and openness to agile behaviors. Pure IQ and past successes are not enough. Nor are strategies any longer proprietary but are now market-based, with digital underpinnings that don't wait for leaders who cannot master the agility to act with urgency.

In my classes of thirty leaders, the most common questions have focused on strategic agility. They have asked why, with the escalation of digitalization and renewed strategies during the past two pandemic-impacted years, do leaders lag in pace and not embrace this capability? Is it lack of agility? Slow pace appears to be the biggest impediment to success. It is attributed to the leader's mindset – in particular, to how they can adapt to the reality that strategies do have a shelf life no matter how successful they were in the past. Moreover, the market doesn't wait: fast, agile action is essential.

Leaders must therefore "see around corners," anticipate what lies down the road, and prepare for the unexpected.

The preponderance of caution among leaders is somewhat understandable, especially if one considers the challenge of moving ahead on strategies while at the same time reducing the uncertainty and instability experienced by their teams and all stakeholders. Managing the tension between daily, monthly, and quarterly actions and the longer term is hard. Nevertheless, this much harsher environment is not going away. The leader needs strategic agility, beginning with personal adaptability and overlaid with critical thinking.

Anticipating Risk

Tiff Macklem speaks insightfully of strategic agility, of "seeing ahead" while anticipating risk:

> Both the global financial crisis, and before that the Great Depression, illustrate the knock-on effect of decisions taken during difficult times; they can inadvertently trigger outcomes not intended or fully anticipated. The global financial crisis triggered a sovereign debt crisis in Europe and fueled a rise in populism in many Western countries. That's why leaders must think today of what tomorrow's problem will be. You have to get ahead of crises to stop them.

Janice Gross Stein adds further insights on short-termism and risk signals:

> Risk is part and parcel of strategic agility. Thinking ahead means you don't have perfect knowledge of the future; whatever strategy you pursue will inevitably have risk. As I learned from a Standard Oil

CEO many years ago, the challenge for leaders is thinking two to three years ahead, not today. For most of us, thinking five years ahead is almost impossible. Could anyone in 2018 have anticipated where we are today in a global pandemic, for example?

Janice also connects strategic agility with problem-solving when others are stymied:

A senior CEO in the health sector had an institutional problem – a high rate of "fall statistics" at the hospital. Some board members proposed an inclusive group from all levels of staff, including housekeepers and maintenance, to try and solve this problem. The group was asked – if you were trying to maximize the rate of falls, what would you do? A housekeeper said she'd wash the floor at 9:00 a.m. when all medical staff were doing their rounds. Within thirty minutes solutions were found in a dozen areas. Move people out of the box they're in. When they look in from outside, they see solutions.

Both personal adaptability and strategic agility rely on a leader having an open mindset. Strategic agility can sometimes be less demanding in that many people typically buy into a strategy and can influence others more readily than when it is about a personal individual adaptability.

What It Takes to Be More Strategically Agile

Requirements	Actions – Behaviors
❖ Interpreting trends	❖ Letting go of the tried and true
❖ Market-based understanding	❖ A mindset of three As:
❖ Dynamic vs. static decisions	• Appraising constantly
❖ Avoiding inaction	• Adjusting courageously
❖ Being locked into familiarity	• Acting urgently

CHAPTER FOURTEEN

The Big 8 #3: Self-Renewal

It Starts with Mindset

The entire theme of this book relates to leaders embracing ongoing learning, beginning in the early chapters of parts 1 and 2 with the case for why this is required. In crystalizing the Big 8 capabilities, self-renewal emerges as a critical capability fundamental to leading in these extraordinary times.

Renewing self is rooted in a leader's own willingness; no one else can supply it. Like personal adaptability and strategic agility, it is owned and can only be exercised by the leader themself. Thus, it is the leader's state of mind (or mindset) that enables self-renewal. If a leader has a fixed or closed mindset, these three capabilities can remain substandard and impossible to master. As Ralph Nader once said: "There is nothing worse than a teacher who is unteachable."

Seizing Opportunities to Learn

Leadership is *not* timeless – that is the reality. The circumstances that help leaders get to where they are change constantly.

Therefore, keeping up and staying relevant is pretty well mandatory if one wants to be a valuable and effective leader. Fortunately, we do see evidence of leaders initiating or seizing opportunities to renew their skills and increase their knowledge, as they shift their mindsets to a more open and current stance. This is confirmed through personal observation and by organizations that are investing heavily in executive development for their top leaders, not just the middle managers. It is further evident in the stories shared throughout this book by such wonderfully accomplished leaders. These leaders speak passionately of their own ongoing learning, the turning points of their journey, and their discovery that they needed to do things differently in order to adapt and renew constantly.

Renewal Is a Journey

Why, then, you might ask, does self-renewal warrant a dedicated chapter and a place in the Big 8 if many leaders are already committed to it? Fair question. It is because we need so much more of it! We need every leader, including the most accomplished – and especially these, because they are the role models – to set the tone, as their impact on others is far reaching. Emerging leaders must see this as the norm; it is the criterion for leader worthiness. Recall Darryl White's concerns about the knock-on effects of having a poor or uninformed or unsuitable leader in place.

In many firsthand discussions in boardrooms, when leadership potential and succession are the key topics, I frequently hear the words "if only." "If only this leader had been told sooner" or "if only she undertook to adjust her thinking or behaviors or even to upgrade her skills and knowledge." It is sad when this comes too late and potential promotions are lost because of a candidate's deficiencies in underdeveloped capabilities. Seeing this lost potential and the loss of opportunity for someone's dreams has inspired me to examine how to change such scenarios.

More Self-Awareness Is Key

The biggest hurdle that leaders need to overcome is their low levels of self-awareness. This is one of the most common blind spots in even the most accomplished and successful of leaders. Sometimes I've wondered how much greater a leader could be with increased self-awareness. Self-awareness is an ingredient for each of the Big 8 and, for those who embrace it, an enabler of effective self-renewal. Generic or ad hoc (instinctive) assumptions about ongoing learning is yesterday's thinking. Feedback, mentors, being teachable through an open mind are now the criteria for self-renewal actions – all part of intentional leadership and going well beyond instinct.

So how does a leader become more self-aware? The answer starts with the impact (positive or negative) that leaders have on those around them. What could be adjusted for greater positive impact? How can the leader connect and communicate with others in various situations? It is surprising how even the smartest leaders who might mean well have little idea of their true impact.

Tiff Macklem tells of his own learning related to the fragility of how leaders connect with others, especially their teams:

Self-awareness can also come from defining moments. One such moment came from my approach to board meetings at the Bank of Canada, as the senior deputy governor. These meetings were always very organized, process-oriented, agenda-driven. I always felt I was there to answer questions, present solutions – singlehandedly know it all – and get the board to approve management's recommendations. Then a senior director took me aside and suggested I needed to change my attitude to board meetings. I shouldn't see it as all about gaining approvals. Instead, I should regard the meetings as an opportunity to benefit from highly experienced board members who were predisposed to my success and the organization's success – both went together. These people are all working for you. The light bulb went on. Since then, I have really engaged the boards of the organizations I have run, including creating advisory boards for the purpose of tapping into an undetected treasure trove of goodwill and experience. Building a protective wall around singularity of focus may make you overlook the rich resources at hand. Sometimes the safest place to go is right in front of you – if you open your eyes and your mind.

Tiff's story emphasizes open-mindedness – that is, having the mindset of enhancing one's way of connecting. It means moving from a more common question-and-answer approach in order to obtain approval to an open, listening, consultative, and inclusive approach. This enabled him to gain rich learning he might not otherwise have had.

Know Your Blind Spots

To illustrate the importance of self-awareness and knowing one's blind spots, Janice Gross Stein describes a personal realization of how she regarded rules:

Self-awareness and knowledge of one's own deficits are important. I admit I have always found rule-following too slow, too constricting. Instead, I tend to see a way around the rules. This is both an asset and a deficit, as it's risky. For those who take action, they automatically take risk. Of course, too much risk can destroy confidence in what you're doing, your team, your project. So where do you live on this asset-deficit continuum? How do you achieve the balance? For me, it's about finding the most risk-averse and law-abiding person possible. Put that person in the number two spot with the job of telling me that I'm putting the whole enterprise at risk and what I should do to mitigate the risks I'm creating. That's how I use self-awareness to manage my "deficit."

The poignant point in Janice's story is the leader's role in utilizing the strengths of others, recognizing that no one leader has all the answers, nor do all leaders need to acquire all capabilities equally. Successful leaders like Janice are self-aware, they understand their blind spots, and they build a team in light of this self-awareness. In this way, they enhance not only their presence and their leadership but also provide a role model for the team. The mistake often made is when a leader does not recognize the blind spot or, much worse, to recognize the blind spot or shortcoming and do nothing about it. When that occurs, the leader, the organization, and the teams all suffer.

Self-Image Is Not Self-Awareness

Self-awareness is not the same as having self-image. Self-awareness is created by objective, candid, and helpful feedback. That's the reason it's powerful for making adjustments, as well as being very helpful when promoted or taking on a new assignment. It is about "knowing what you do not know." This is always watched for in new leaders, especially when they expand and inherit new or larger teams and gain wider leadership responsibilities. Meric Gertler elaborates on this point in a perspective from his personal journey:

When I became dean of arts and science at the University of Toronto, I was faced with a quantum leap in scope and scale of leadership expectations compared to what I'd experienced before – with 30,000 students, 1,000 faculty, plus administrative and maintenance staff. Now, in an academic setting, a familiar question arose. How do you get people to do what you want them to? How do you organize the team so that we all become collectively impactful and focused on goals? It took a lot of tinkering and adjusting. The university, as an organization, had outgrown the capacity of the dean's office to manage it. The expectation of leadership in academic institutions was to have a vision, supported by strategies and a plan. But it was unrealistic just to dictate a plan, hand it to people, and expect them to do your bidding. I became obsessed with the challenge of getting people to think your idea is theirs and gain buy-in. Of course, success did not come right away. Mistakes were made. A brilliant plan developed in a vacuum landed with a thud when it came to implementation. In hindsight, such results were entirely predictable. I was learning on the job. I realized I had to slow down, back up, engage with key constituencies across the faculty in a more meaningful way. By listening more carefully and working to find common ground with recalcitrant faculty, I was ultimately able to convince them to join in supporting the plan.

Meric's story is not uncommon. One hears presidents, CEOs, and senior leaders lament: "If only I had learned this much earlier. I wonder if a mentor or the insights of trusted others would have been helpful along the way." Of course, we know that mentors are helpful and that the path to leadership might have been less stressful than it was. It is lonely at the top. Learning from others does help, as I personally found out when I had falsely assumed that I was expected to have all the answers (as described in chapter 10). A mentor can help you recognize this wrong assumption and make your journey less difficult – and less unnecessarily stressful. This comes with self-awareness, intentionality, and renewal.

Picking Your Spots for Renewal

Marc-André Blanchard offers a perspective on having a mindset that identifies the actual points in time for renewal:

> Leadership evolves – and so do you. Along the way you add experience and learn from experiences – especially transformational leadership. You have to identify the time for transformation as well as have the courage to execute the necessary actions. For example, twenty years ago, I led the restructuring of the McCarthy Tetrault partnership. This was the biggest undertaking of my professional career. It was an awful task to have to ask one-quarter of the partnership to leave the firm in order to give space for the young talent that was growing. Yet it had to be done. Today, two decades later, the results are there for all to see.

Having a mindset that is open to learning from experience and feedback is imperative in becoming more self-aware. But this needs to be coupled with having the courage to adjust and try new or difficult ways – in other words, to act. Mentorship can be the catalyst for both. As Ron Farmer points out: "You have to have access to coaches or mentors, gain feedback and have a relationship of trust with them. Those jobs at the top are very lonely." Leadership is strengthened when you have such access. This should be thought of more often.

It's Hard! Leadership Is Hard

It's hard to continuously self-renew. And if you are a CEO, it's hard to look to the chair of the board for advice. But mentors can be an answer if carefully chosen. Self-awareness in leadership can be enhanced when built on a strong foundation with all who provide feedback. The key is that the feedback should be relevant, objective, and impactful. But this leads to further questions about self-awareness, feedback, and mentoring. For example, how can you gain feedback without appearing insecure or vulnerable or without embarrassment? How can you anticipate the challenges of being thrown in the deep end through promotion and unpreparedness? And how does one adjust behavior without looking silly?

Curiosity and Intention Help

In my own leadership experiences, learning does come from mistakes and from admitting to not having all the answers. Becoming teachable and open and being around other great insightful people, including mentors, has helped me tremendously. Having a need to know things and a continuing curiosity also feed teachability. Whether it comes from innate curiosity or through intentionality – either is welcome and impactful in becoming a better leader. I find inspiration in Katie Taylor's story about her ongoing self-reinvention:

> At university, I learned that women could do many other things – be professors, authors, and so forth – and switched to political science and economics. Thus began the process of "reinventing myself." I went to post-graduate school, specializing in law and business. After meeting a woman investment banker, my aspirations changed. Despite seeing women in these roles, it wasn't until later that I started to see women in leadership. In my early years, there weren't many role models. Fortunately, while at Four Seasons, I got a front row seat to see what leadership looked like. Observing the renowned hotelier,

Issy Sharp, and how he worked was the beginning of my thinking about leadership and what worked best for companies. I learned how to trust and delegate. I discovered that *influence* was most important in leadership, not control. You have to stand for things, for values and purposes, and "lead through power of example, not power of position." People have followed me because they know I stand for good things and am open about it.

Leaders Are Always Role-Modeling

On role-modeling as a powerful means of self-renewal, Mary Jo Haddad offers an interesting and helpful perspective:

Sometimes you can answer that question by talking about leaders you haven't understood or respected. What often lies at the root of disaffection is a difference in values. Perhaps that person wasn't grounded in the same values as you. However, that may be clouding your judgment and you might be missing a more balanced appreciation of the person's leadership. Rather than pass judgment, start with one's own self-reflection; it teaches you to be honest with yourself. Ask yourself: what are my skills and capabilities and what aren't? Keep your mind open; check your stance. Surround yourself with people who can bolster you and provide the skills you don't have. In that way, we as leaders become role models for others. A grounding in different values is not in itself a showstopper; rather, it's what you see and act on following self-reflection. Staying honest in knowing your limitations, taking steps to have counter-balancing influence from others around you – this will do more for successful leadership. Allow yourself to be open enough to get feedback and criticism. As a leader, what I do today will have an impact on and influence others. Keeping this in mind is the way to start every day.

These testimonies and real-time experiences will help reinforce why self-renewal is such an imperative; why it must occupy its own place and prominence in the priorities of every leader and in the BIG 8; and why it is fundamentally enabled by the leader's own mindset.

What It Takes to Be Focused on Self-Renewal

Requirements	Actions – Behaviors
❖ A mindset for learning	❖ Seeking feedback
❖ Not assuming you have all the answers	❖ Knowing your own blind spots (self-awareness)
❖ Dispelling "once a leader, always a leader" view	❖ Being teachable
❖ Unlocked from yesterday's assumptions	❖ Leading with intention

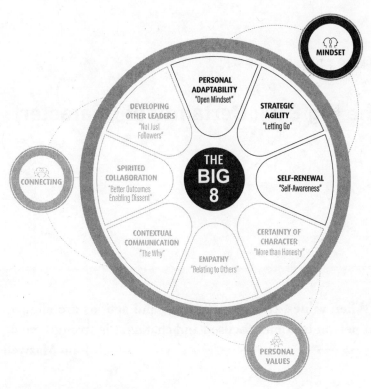

FIGURE 15. The Big 8: Mindset

CHAPTER FIFTEEN

The Big 8 #4: Certainty of Character

When values, thoughts, feelings and actions are aligned,
a person becomes focused and character is strengthened.

John Maxwell

It Starts with Personal Values

Everyone owns their character and is responsible for it. Character is not a victim of circumstances; it survives in spite of them. Yet there is still a resistance to, or kind of silence around, codifying character as a top capability for leaders and speaking to it regularly. After the global financial crisis, certainty of character emerged quickly as needing more emphasis and explicit attention among the Big 8. The first time I cited it in my teaching, it met with some pause, almost an awkward reaction. This was not because the leaders in the class did not agree with its importance, but because it was most often just assumed – at least until there were early warning signals or indicators being detected. Even then, it was put into the category of "tedious" and "difficult to confront."

Regulatory scrutiny and constant evidence of fraud, deception, and wrongdoing have combined to shine a light on character. It is often thought of as honesty and not often as an explicit item in a leader's list of capabilities. In examining the traits, values, and virtues distinguishing successful companies from those that failed during the global financial crisis, the Richard Ivey School of Business was one of the first to seriously acknowledge character as a key factor in a leader's qualification. This finding resulted in development of a character framework. I commend the Ivey School for its initiative and for the quality and courage it showed in the published conclusions.[1]

Character Is More than Honesty

The Big 8 defines character as beyond lying or stealing. It is that, of course, but much more if we look to becoming and remaining a worthy leader. There is much attention now being given to character in the context of leadership – one recent article that captures informative research is Ayesha Dey's "When Hiring CEOS, Focus on Character: Personal Behaviour Can Predict which Leaders Might Go Astray."[2] As noted above, everyone owns their character and is responsible for it. Character is powered by a leader's core values; it reflects the depth and breadth of who they are and what they stand for in any circumstance, regardless of its demands. Organizations have made statements of core values for many years; they are explicit in mission statements and ethics policies. This is all well and good and most welcome. But the explicit meaning of character and its certainty within the Big 8 is underpinned by the individual values of a leader. While the latter can be influenced and even shaped by the organization's values, they are nonetheless owned, expressed, and lived by each leader – through the earning and re-earning of trust and through truth and transparency.

At the essence of character are the three Ts: truth, trust, and transparency. Everyone expects these in a leader, and decisions and judgments about leaders are made on whether or not they possess this certainty of character. The current pandemic has confirmed that certainty of character is now expected as table stakes, a fact further confirmed by accomplished leaders in the conversations shared in this book.

Barry Perry speaks of certainty of character as "having honor in the game" and "having an obligation to do the right thing." This starts with the obligation of the CEO, who sets the tone, to do the right thing. He relates how he took an important lesson from the experience of leading one of the biggest acquisitions done by Fortis. After the deal was put to bed, Barry ran into new problems that could have caused him to reconsider. However, he didn't and instead managed them by restructuring parts of the deal. Why didn't he jump ship and abandon the deal in light of the new problems? He felt it wasn't the right thing to do. "It's hard to turn back once you are deep into a deal. Being in the trenches with lots of pressure while still doing the right thing takes both character, strength, and principles." When asked what propelled him through the difficult choices in such circumstances where there were no other bidders and he had other options, including turning back, he says: "Word and commitment, once given are your honor." It was about trust, fairness, and keeping his word through transparency and truth – the essence of character.

Doing the Right Thing Daily

For many years at the BMO Financial Group, the many ways of "doing the right thing" was taught. It was reinforced through a policy called "first principles." Every employee, including directors of the board, had to sign a protocol annually to confirm their adherence

to the principles, which posed three questions when making decisions: Is it fair? Is it right? Is it legal? This example speaks to character in the sense of decision-making. However, the Big 8 requires leaders to go look farther, beyond the **Is it fair?**
Is it right?
Is it legal?
decision-making questions, and examine how they earn trust with stakeholders daily. Employees and other stakeholders gauge trust by many day-to-day encounters. What do they look for in assessing a leader's character? The Big 8 identifies five ways in which leaders are rated for character. These five checks can (and should) guide a leader's mindset, thoughts, and actions and become a barometer of how a leader intentionally leads every day.

Values – More than Personality Traits

Every leader who has shared stories for this book has zeroed in on the expectations placed on leaders for earning daily and sustained trust. Katie Taylor, for instance, expresses it this way:

> [I know] how hugely important such leadership values are – not as personality traits but as skills acquired and values firmly held. Many such skills are learned along the way. It doesn't matter if a leader is an extravert or introvert; it is how you show up, how you engage, how you treat people. At heart, "trust" is the "currency of leadership." Trust comes in many ways. People have to believe in you. It's not "once and done": you have to prove your worth again and again. Leaders need to be thoughtful, therefore, about how they solve problems when others are watching and also when they're not. Everyone is looking – as well as when people are not looking. To engender trust, especially in a crisis, you have to earn it every day and with every interaction.

Taking Personal Responsibility!

Tiff Macklem relates character and trust to taking personal responsibility and ensuring that decisions, whether large or small in impact, are not made at the expense of others. "This is what integrity means. Integrity does not lie solely in carrying out official job responsibilities or assuming the accountabilities assigned by the organization's mandate. Integrity also lies in staying balanced in behavior toward those around you, able to show vulnerability and coachability, always keeping an even keel, not showing irritation." Leaders' discussions and choices are tough. While processes are often in place to guide decision-making, sometimes those alone are not enough. Quiet determination, fortitude, and concern for all affected by decisions are needed.

Certainty of Character Begins with the Three Ts: Truth, Trust, and Transparency

Five indicators to watch for in leaders' behavior:

- Keeping your word (*Integrity*)
- Looking to self for cause (*Responsibility*)
- Sticking neck out (*Courage*)
- Letting go of others' mistakes (*Forgiveness*)
- Putting self in others' shoes (*Empathy*)

Character will always be focused on honesty, of course. However, for leaders who are role models, who are entrusted with the privilege of guiding others, who need to show their worthiness every day – their character and trust are undergoing a closer look through such fine lenses. This is what all the stakeholders across our society at large are looking for each day. Even though you don't always know when you see it, digging deeper in order to confirm certainty of standards and indicators of character is now the norm.

CHAPTER SIXTEEN

The Big 8 #5: Empathy

I think we all have empathy, but we may not have the courage to display it.

Maya Angelou

It Starts with Personal Values

A while back, I was invited to teach the framework of the Big 8 to military personnel in an international leadership exchange. Initially, I wondered whether I was the right person to accept the invitation. I assumed that "command and control" was their predominant leadership tenet, whereas my approach to leadership was all about "connect and collaborate." They assured me, yes, I was what they wanted. They recognized that broader and evolving leadership is an intentional addition to what is expected of a leader. Of course, command and control would be a core principle in their management models. But leadership in its broadest sense called for more. They were shining the light on this reality and included the Big 8 as being highly relevant.

I Didn't Know It Was Called Empathy!

As the session proceeded, I was elaborating on empathy and what it means and how it fits in every leader's role and success. After giving examples of empathetic actions of leaders – such as listening well, relating to another person's feelings, seeing through another's eyes – I asked the class: "In your daily activity, do you as a leader ever intentionally take this mindset and relate to others in this way?" A field officer's hand went up: "Oh yes, I do all the time; but I didn't know it was called empathy!" Henry (we will call him) is one of the effective leaders who uses empathy naturally. We see this happening daily and we recognize the positive impact it creates for others. These leaders typically have strong core values and care about the other person(s), putting themselves in their shoes.

Empathy needs far more understanding than the misguided interpretations held by many. Common misgivings about empathy in organizational environments typically include three groups of mindsets:

- Group one: Those who believe empathy is a soft skill and more compatible with personal relationships/friendships and less compatible with workplace requirements, especially from leaders. Policies are intended to be caring and considerate to address it.
- Group two: Those who worry that people will expect too much. It will require exceptions and leaders will be taken advantage of.
- Group three: Those who do not consciously resist, but just do not understand the power of empathy and how both the leader and those receiving empathy can benefit.

Today, we hear so much more about the absence of empathy in leaders. It is now being recognized somewhat more as an essential capability for leaders. However, more rigor is needed in calling for it in leaders who are lacking this capability. Moreover, leaders own empathy. It cannot be automated or outsourced to others, although far too often it is assumed to be the primary role of human resources professionals.

> Empathy is one of the greatest tools of business leadership that is most underused.
>
> Steven Covey

Empathy Enables Horizontal Leadership

In an early chapter, we reviewed the concept of "T" leadership. It responded to the need for leading across boundaries (horizontal leadership), increasing collaboration across units and projects, and going well beyond "silo-ism." From this shift from the vertical to the horizontal, which has been one of the hardest for leaders, empathy has emerged as an important means of helping leaders connect better with employees and stakeholders. Tiff Macklem speaks of empathy in the context of "the people element of leading":

> The people element cannot be secondary to the technical. When dealing with crisis, think about how it will be perceived and how people will react, rather than purely technical solutions. When a major bank is in trouble and the public authorities come in with a technical solution and fix it, you might expect that to be reassuring. But that's often not how the average person reacts. They are thinking, if this large bank just failed, who's next? Is my bank going to fail? Even the best technical solutions often don't restore public confidence.

Instead, you must consider how the information from your decisions and actions is going to be received by people. What will be the impact on their behavior as a result? Recall, for example, that the bank bailouts of the global financial crisis were greeted by public resentment that translated into an increase in populist support.

Tiff's point is about how a leader makes people feel, similar to the Maya Angelou quote at the beginning of the chapter. He also illuminates the essence of empathy as putting oneself in another's shoes – how will any average person react to a situation?

Post–COVID-19 Drives Greater Compassion

Showing concern for others in the workforce has become even more critical in this post-pandemic time. We see leaders everywhere grappling with many unprecedented decisions, such as when to decide that people should return to the workplace. This invokes the risk of leaders assuming what employees want and would prefer – a risk that can be mitigated by empathy. This is one of the reasons that the expectation for leaders is increasingly focused on strong human skills and why empathy and compassion have explicitly risen to the top of expectations and is watched closely.

Meric Gertler believes the University of Toronto and its key leaders will adopt and respond to these new demands, because the foundations and beliefs guiding their approach to employee care are based on the principles of empathy. Showing care for employees can be done, as Meric notes, through recognition of the importance of work-life balance and vacations that are taken, not skipped. Responding to a question about the physical and mental health of employees in the post–COVID-19 environment, he further notes:

Working during holiday time is a deeply ingrained behavior at
U of T. For some of our VPs and academics, doing research is almost
the same as a holiday. They regard it as a refreshing change, a time to
flex different mental muscles. It's hard to dislodge this behavior, but
important to do so. Today, U of T is recognized as one of Canada's
top employers with a rich array of benefits – including vacation.

Empathy Cannot Be Outsourced or Automated

Such stories tell us that displaying empathy and caring is every leader's job. It is especially critical that leaders at the top set the tone by
their big decisions as well as their individual smaller decisions and
through their personal interactions each day. Katie Taylor reaffirms
this aspect of empathy and its display through small everyday actions. She calls it empathetic leadership.

> The biggest impact on my approach to leadership came from watch-
> ing how senior leaders interacted with company employees. Some
> were gruff, harsh – and this had impact on people. I saw others who
> always took time to have coffee and chat with employees. One in
> particular, the head of global hotel operations, would have morning
> coffee everyday with the overnight shoeshine man. This person made
> leadership tangible for me. I saw his impact on the business – he was
> incredibly trusted and highly respected, able to touch people in all
> walks of life, whether on big or small issues. I saw it even in his letters
> and how he changed small things such as "enjoyed talking with you"
> (not *to* you). I found his approach very powerful and adopted it.

Maya Angelou said: "I think we all have empathy, but we may not
have the courage to display it." Like many others, my own initial
worry about displaying empathy was its potential to convey an image

of being too soft and amenable. Thanks to the great work in the late 1990s of Daniel Golman's work related to EQ, I learned how impactful it was for a leader to enhance and display empathy. This was further reinforced through positive feedback from others (over 100 emails!) who were acknowledging my empathetic approach. This increased my courage, my comfort, and my intention to ensure that I practiced it deliberately. Empathy is now at the top of my advice and priorities. It clearly holds a place of prominence in the Big 8 for a leader's success.

Just like certainty of character, empathy is powered by core values. Both are dependent on strong values of personal responsibility for who you are, what you stand for, and your obligation to uphold the worthiness of being a leader. Just as a leader owns their character – no matter what the circumstances – a leader also is the only one who can be empathetic to those they lead. To repeat: empathy cannot be automated or outsourced.[1]

Empathy – The Leader's Individual Ability to Relate to Others

Requirements	Actions – Behaviors
❖ Tuning into other individuals	❖ Being open, accessible, approachable
❖ Putting self in others' shoes	❖ Showing self-awareness
❖ Relating to the feelings of others	❖ Knowing impact on others
❖ Unlocked from yesterday's assumptions	❖ Adjusting behavior in order to relate

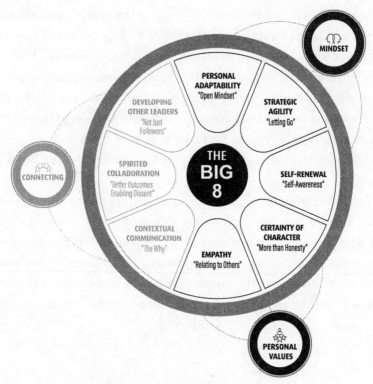

FIGURE 16. The Big 8: Mindset and Personal Values

CHAPTER SEVENTEEN

The Big 8 #6: Contextual Communication

It Starts with Connecting

In today's extraordinary times, leaders are keen to know what motivates their teams; so, too, are teams eager to understand their leaders' motivations. The simple answer is for leaders to explain "the why" and the purpose – and not assume it is self-evident.

Effective communication always appears on any list of leadership skills, whether it is one of ten or one of fifty on the list. Yet, in most organizations, communication is rated lower in most surveys. *Why?* It is, in fact, the absence of "the why" that is the very reason for this inadequacy. Communicating without "the why," without the purpose, but with just "the what" doesn't do it in today's workforce. The view of all teams across the organization is that they deserve to know "the why" and the purpose, and to have some input in some way, even if only through questions and comments to the leader.

Quickly Formed Views

The quick access to knowledge and other data points through both social media and increasingly enhanced technology is enabling people to form their own views and preconceived ideas. The leaders' challenge and their obligation are to make sense of an issue by first explaining its context within a specific organization. In other words, explaining "the why" the goal makes sense, not just *what* the goal is. This is not always self-evident – so why leave it to chance?

Unfortunately, even great leaders communicate *what* they believe the audience merely needs to know or to be told! Isn't that the most important and the most expedient? This is often the common mindset for leaders. Yet few would argue that intentional leadership is about (a) getting teams to rally around the plans and goals; (b) getting people to offer discretionary energy that goes above and beyond the job description; and (c) getting them to understand the importance of the purpose and vision. This is successful leading!

The question, then, is, What do leaders need to do differently to enhance the effectiveness of their communication and their engagement with others? A leader's ability to tune into new and different mindsets and put aside yesterday's assumptions is in full demand more than ever. So much has changed in terms of today's workforce and stakeholders. Expectations are very different, but this is not yet grasped by many senior leaders.

It's Not Just "the What" – It's Also "the Why"

One significant and encompassing expectation across all audiences and society at large is the desire and appetite to understand "the why" behind a leader's motivations and decisions. We say this in the unmistakable game changer of stakeholder expectations and its relationship to truth, trust, and transparency. It was again a critical capability in the unmistakable game changer of short-lived strategies. Alignment by everyone to strategies is always about "the why" and not just "the what." This will capture people and engage them, building trust and buy-in. And it is most certainly true in the unmistakable game changer of the changing workforce and workplace. Since the work on the Big 8 began, much has been written about the practice of engaging employees and others. Books and articles and insights have been offered. But communication still stands as an impediment to greater success. Why is that?

The importance of "the why" prevails at every step in arriving at each of the Big 8 and is the premise for this book. It begins with part 1 by discerning why leadership is harder through the unmistakable game changers and then, in part 2, by exploring why a leader's own mindset sometimes is their biggest impediment. All of which leads to the leader's ability to really tune into new and different challenges and to recognize their teams' potential, their energy and engagement. While each of the Big 8 is equally critical and intertwined in this big purpose of leaders, communication becomes paramount. It is about communicating the context, "the why"; about translating the problem into *purpose* and thereby into the actions considered most appropriate.

The Magic of Telling "the Why"

Mary Jo Haddad has already offered (in chapter 6) that communicating the *why* demonstrates a leader's openness and accessibility. This goes beyond the perceived disconnect that can appear with leaders who are more closed-minded and only tell *what* is to be done/accomplished. Marc-André Blanchard provides another good example of the pitfall encountered when "the why" is not explained:

A key aspect of leadership is the capability to communicate. Some years ago, our firm was moving offices to a new ultra-modern building in Montreal and I inherited leading the project. Though initially against it, I now had to make it happen. A year later, while moving in, I heard my own assistant tell a client that nobody had consulted the employees, who liked the old place and were unhappy. What I realized was that, while the project was well executed, the communication about it was awful. I immediately undertook presentations to employees to boost the mood and acceptance of the move. The lesson I learned? You can do operations well, but if you don't communicate well, you're in trouble.

Marc-André's experience is a common happening arising from not getting feedback or input to begin with. This is exactly the reality when initial communication is without context, leaving a total void for employees. Yes, the project can get done, but how much the better could it have been done *if* employees understood "the why" this path was chosen and had an opportunity to ask questions or express their views? Employees and stakeholders do not expect to change the course of action or the leader's decision, but today, they expect to be heard and expect their voices to be of value.

Why Means Context

Tiff Macklem emphasizes the importance of communicating the context:

In communicating leadership, the sequence of questions to be addressed is vital. The first question is "the why." What's the purpose of the work at hand? If you get people excited about "the why," they'll give you all they've got. From there, proceed to "the who" – that is, build the team around you, using the value of diversity of thought and approach to get the best advice possible. Then, thirdly, decide on "the what" – the action resulting from the decision taken, now collectively executed by the team acting as one.

Notwithstanding evidence that many leaders are renewing their capabilities in communicating and engaging, I still see frequent situations where the leader misses the context when communicating. What is so often seen is a big focus on clarifying "the what," then persuading people as to "the how." This leaves employees or other audiences with their own preconceived ideas or views – none of which were heard. Consequently, engagement, if not productivity, will be suboptimal for sure.

Why Means Trust

People do not automatically buy into "the what" or "the how," but they do buy into "the why," and do so much more often. What is missing is (a) why it matters to do something, (b) to whom it matters, and (c) the employees' role in making it matter. More than an expression of respect, communicating "the why" engenders trust! Taking time to offer "the why," to explain the context and hear viewpoints, results in the act of empathizing. It conveys that the leader is allowing humanity to be present. Even though a leader's role is to explain the logic and analytics that appeal to the person's mind, "the why" appeals to the (heart) feelings and to the attitude. Hearts as well as heads matter today.

It is common to believe that such personable communication can happen more in small companies or family businesses than within larger organizations. This is an outdated and highly impeding belief. Of course, formal systems, data-based decisions, and logical quantitative frameworks are not only important but also are better enabled today with technology. This enables leaders to be smarter in their analyses and conclusions – facts are still favored! However, a concern is that leaders resist taking the time to communicate more holistically by engaging others in this more human, respectful, and contextual fashion. Too much reliance on formal systems, scripted presentations of decisions, and forms of flow-down connections from senior layers of leadership will *not* harness the true energy of today's workforce, nor will it tap into their true potential.

"The Why" Means Connecting Better

The accessibility of leaders and the power of personal individual connection enable leaders to listen better. Listening is now the gold standard: it is the champion of inclusion. It sets an important and valued cultural norm. One revealing action that leaders can take to see how their communication is landing is to walk around and listen to what is being discussed through informal channels. This will tell a leader about employee assumptions. Walking around can often provide leaders with much richer information and insights than the responses on the usual paper-based surveys and questionnaires.

Barry Perry speaks passionately about how accessibility and listening drives his company's leadership:

> You have to realize that fifteen years ago Fortis didn't have all the functions of communications and investor relations. We had to build them up ourselves. It required connecting with people. You had to get out and meet people. For the companies we bought, it required telling them "your culture is yours, we're not going to interfere with it." Through this process of treating people with respect, Fortis created a cohesive organization that appears to have a very strong culture

right across the board. It was amazing to see. We bought businesses, put them together without changing them – and they've somehow all grown together into one unit.

For Barry, this way of connecting with employees is built on inclusiveness and accessibility, the basis of collaboration and buy-in. The previous chapter on empathy and this chapter on contextual communication are essential for what collaboration means in today's organizations.

And as we will see in the next chapter, the seventh capability – spirited collaboration – strengthens this essential quality of leadership.

Contextual Communication – Making Sense with "the Why"

Requirements	Actions – Behaviors
❖ Allowing questions	❖ Relating to logic *and* feelings
❖ Listening more than talking	❖ Going beyond the analytical mindset to consider emotions
❖ Explaining "the why"	❖ Understanding others' states of mind by recognizing preconceived mindsets
❖ Translating complexity	

CHAPTER EIGHTEEN

The Big 8 #7: Spirited Collaboration

It Starts with Connecting

Spirited collaboration has a big and critical place in intentional leadership!

- It is not a choice – it is a necessity.
- It is a means – not an end.
- It welcomes dissent – not just consensus.
- It is always inclusive and boundaryless – not just vertical!

Concepts of collaboration have been much promoted in leadership literature in recent years. My experience at BMO, where collaboration was introduced as a core value, contributed to the decision to coin it in the Big 8 as "spirited collaboration." Why "spirited"? Because it was not clear what "collaboration" meant!

Collaboration conjures up a variety of myths and assumptions. However, what I call "spirited collaboration" stands strong among the Big 8, not as a choice but as a must if one is to succeed in these

extraordinary times. Our three unmistakable game changers –
stakeholder expectations, the changing workforce and workplace,
and digitalization – call for it. The pendulum shift is moving *from*
command and control *to* connect and collaborate. Yet it is still dis-
counted, if not at times dismissed, by those who believe that collaboration requires endless meetings, that it lets people off the hook by
disguising accountability, that it's all about harmony and being nice
to get consensus!

Collaboration – Better Outcomes, Not Echo Chambers

This latter perception of collaboration relates to my own experience
more than a decade ago at BMO. Collaborating, as one of our four
core values, was completely welcomed, becoming part of everyone's
performance evaluation. But soon executives consulted with me for
advice on the misalignment they saw with collaboration. "Rose,"
they asked, "this corporate value of collaboration is not being practiced by many – so how can it be a value if it's not upheld?" This was
an important question. My response was: "Tell me what you are observing or encountering." And their stories all pointed to my saying:
"Oh, you mean they're not 'agreeing' with others – or with you!"

My response prompted a review of how we had – or rather had
not – explained why collaboration was so critical to leading well, to
executing on strategy, and to harnessing energy and getting alignment of teams. From this emerged the true meaning of collaboration: "achieving a better outcome." To do so requires dissent and
needs it to be allowed. It requires diverse opinions and needs them
to be heard. All this gave way to "spirited collaboration" – enabling
and encouraging dissent, with the ultimate objective of arriving at a
better outcome. A harmonious group of like minds becomes an echo
chamber of agreement. A leader who doesn't allow diverse opinions

and ideas for improvement will perform suboptimally. Today's leadership challenges – a more complex and diverse workplace, digitalization, far-reaching stakeholder expectations – will push the need for inclusive and dissenting ("spirited") collaboration.

Earlier, Ron Farmer spoke of the challenges faced by incoming CEOs who don't have the luxury of time to get plans developed and change accepted via traditional vertical and horizontal structures. It prompts other methods of leadership that come under the banner of "spirited" collaboration. Leading in today's world, Ron says, "needs to include teams, networks, informal relationships; it needs colleagues who can informally act as brokers; it requires building bridges between subgroups operating in white spaces, spotting unsung heroes, and tapping into underutilized talent." Such knowledgeable and highly relevant insights endorse a "spirited" means of collaborating, all connecting to ensure better outcomes. Leadership becomes distributed; the teams are the heroes; and the hierarchical leader becomes the enabler and navigator.

True Collaboration Is Connecting

Spirited, inclusive, and diverse collaboration can take many forms. But, at its essence, it must be intentional, connecting across an organization's internal and external boundaries, defying being locked into vertical leadership units. Instead, ideas, people, and resources not normally or organically linked become connected. When a leader looks horizontally and acts openly, the result is optimal inclusion. In his book *The Tipping Point*, Malcolm Gladwell refers to these people as "connectors" (as discussed in chapter 10). Silos need to be busted. Leaders need to undermine the single-focus, single-accountability approach, although both can and should exist in certain circumstances. In chapter 11, we called the concept of horizontal leadership and connecting across the entire organization "T" leadership. The "T" represents the need to lead with authority in a vertical manner, but now it has become essential to lead horizontally (across units) without full authority. The mastery of co-existing in vertical and horizontal structures relies fully on well-honed collaboration that is diverse and spirited.

Collaboration and Paradoxes

The Center for Creative Leadership (CCL) has declared that "knowing how to manage paradoxes is a game changer." The research is clear: Leaders, teams, individuals, and organizations that manage paradoxes are better performers than those that don't. Having personally been involved in the CCL teachings, I deeply embrace these capabilities. Similarly, being involved in the teachings from research on enterprise leadership done by the Corporate Executive Board (now a part of Gartner) reinforced my beliefs. Practicing spirited collaboration is intentional leadership at its best – and at its hardest.

Among the many leaders connected to the work of the Big 8, we hear stories of spirited collaboration. As Ron Farmer points out, you need it when transforming strategies with purpose and pace:

> Change leadership is very hard if you are leading in a firm that has many attributes that might not be conducive or relevant to work-forces of today and new directions. It is very difficult for CEOs or other incoming leadership to stimulate people and get collaboration that pushes for change. It is not easy to make change happen, despite the proliferation of change management studies. One sees the competing influences of all sorts of groups resisting it, quietly or otherwise; meanwhile, time is of the essence in today's demanding times. It becomes very hard on CEOs trying to push needed change while

managing the high expectations of all stakeholders. This focus on collaboration and getting energy and unity is therefore more critical than ever before.

Culture Can Enhance or Impede Collaboration

Tiff Macklem describes how a leader needs to understand that culture can enhance or impede collaboration within an organization:

A leader must recognize that spirited collaboration takes on a different character depending on the organization and its governance system. I saw this in my transition from the Bank of Canada to the Rotman School of Management. As dean at Rotman, I found I needed to rely more on soft power. The culture and procedures were much more consultative than in the more corporate environment of the Bank of Canada. Instead of influence flowing upwards to rest at the top, the exercise of influence was more distributed. If others besides you have influence too, one cannot move quickly or take control.

However, there's another side of the coin that a leader needs to see. Once the meandering course of decision has reached its end, it's no longer the dean's plan but the faculty's plan. No need therefore to sell it to the faculty. Implementation just happens, because they've been part of the plan all along. There's real value in that process as a leader: the more people see themselves in the plan, the more effective its execution will be. This is important to understand wherever there are other sources of influence beyond one's immediate control. Indeed, I found similarities with international decision-making when I chaired G20 deputies' meetings. The process matters. If everyone believes in the process, decisions will stick and get implemented.

Collaboration Means Listening Well

Meric Gertler places strong emphasis on listening and taking advantage of the input of others. As president of the University of Toronto, he believes it is important to ensure that faculty, staff, and stakeholders know "the why" of specific strategies being taken, which he had learned earlier as a dean: "Do not present ideas as fully baked – people need to be involved, included, and have welcome opportunity to give opposing views." Such an approach leads to a more embraced outcome. Everyone more willingly becomes aligned with the new paths being created. The solid lines on the organizational chart no longer represent the way people actually get the job done.

Meric gives us additional insight into how spirited collaboration works:

A leader needs to demonstrate you're able to listen and are taking account of the input of others. This iterative approach was very important in preparing me for the U of T presidency, where I had to develop a strategic vision for the university. I began having quiet conversations with people around the university, many of whom had recently stepped down as administrators or deans, with some still serving. From that came the "three core ideas" document prepared and released by U of T.

These ideas had to be easily and simply communicated. First, with declining financial support from provincial government grants, the university leadership had to look at every other aspect at their disposal. As an urbanist, I saw the university as integral to Toronto's growth and reputation as a city, but I had to "sell" that to the rest of the university. Second, I emphasized the importance of global engagement at a time when some borders were thickening. The third core idea was the emphasis placed by the university on undergraduate education. This was followed by a year of communicating the three core ideas and asking for feedback. The strategy was unanimously endorsed by the university community, but its success was built on humility. The approach was: "Here's what I think. But tell me what you think. I don't have all the answers." It worked on two levels – first, it gained widespread approval and support; second, by bringing in the ideas of others, we got a better outcome.

Leading with Guiding – Not Control

Increasing adoption of spirited collaboration will no doubt push leaders to operate outside of their formal control. They will need to learn how to inspire with personal connection and how to show greater empathy in relating to others. Spirited collaboration requires strong people skills in depersonalizing ideas, welcoming dissent, and ensuring inputs from others are heard and valued. Not unlike other capabilities in the Big 8, spirited collaboration is hard. But then, leading well today is harder than ever – and it has never been more important.

WAYT? Why Are You Talking?

The threads weaving through the leader's ability to get the team engaged and feeling included through spirited collaboration are threefold. One is "listening by all," but particularly by the leader/navigator. Two is "listening by the team members" to others without discounting or attacking. Three is "listening for understanding." The one fundamental for achieving this is "to be very discerning about your own talking." I have a leader who learned the importance of this by creating a new habit for himself.

Whenever he was in group meeting, he asked himself quietly, "WAYT? Why are you talking?" Our habits of being the leader and displaying it through talking are deeply rooted.

Spirited Collaboration – Better Outcomes by Allowing Dissent

Requirements	Actions – Behaviors
❖ Connecting *across* boundaries	❖ Understanding motivations
❖ Linking ideas, people, resources	❖ Hearing all views
❖ Harnessing differences for a better outcome	❖ Depersonalizing ideas
❖ Encouraging different viewpoints	❖ Allowing and offering dissenting views

CHAPTER NINETEEN

The Big 8 #8: Developing Other Leaders – Not Only Followers

It starts with the premise that the function of leaders is to develop other leaders – not followers.

Ralph Nader

It Starts with Connecting

This leadership capability, the eighth of the Big 8, is about developing other leaders – not merely followers. Shifting the way in which we lead *from* command and control *to* connect and collaborate means that leaders move more to empowerment and distributed leadership in the workplace. Spirited collaboration and inclusiveness, as presented in the previous chapter, contradicts the traditional concept of leader. This does not mean a leader does not lead or inspire or set a purpose within the organization's mission. Of course not – this is the role of a leader! However, given the unmistakable game changers in today's context, the capabilities needed in these extraordinary times differ significantly from what leaders needed earlier. As this book repeatedly asserts: "What got leaders to where they are today has changed."

Preparing Leaders – Improving Practices

Taking responsibility for developing other leaders is not new. It includes one's successor who will outlive the leader's own time. But today it requires different approaches, different commitments, and different obligations. Developing other leaders is part of the worthiness and privilege of being a leader. It goes to the essence of leadership. Here again, the Big 8 reveals what is different from traditional leadership skills and practices. Moreover, it is a call to action for leaders!

In earlier chapters, the less-than-adequate preparation of leaders has been illuminated through the realities of our changing workforce and workplace. We are witnessing disengagement and discontent in the workforce everywhere, and even more so since the COVID-19 pandemic. The motivations and expectations of the workforce are different from what leaders once knew; they have ever more questions. Meanwhile, the practices used by leaders to develop others are no longer as effective, because these were designed based on a different assumption about the relationship between the leader and the team – namely, that there's a leader and all others are followers.

Today's teams are different. Today's teams want to be empowered. They want to have the latitude to impact outcomes and look for purpose to an ever-greater degree. We therefore need to pay more attention to our leadership development commitment and practices. Yet we see an inadequacy in the quantity and quality of the leader supply and in the outlook of the talent pipelines. That is why the Big 8 capability of developing other leaders stands strong among

the other seven capabilities. At the same time, it does not stand sep-
arately, because the Big 8 is a set of overlapping but distinctive capabilities relating to people, harnessing their energy and potential and
helping them to be the best they can be – all for the achievement of
an organization's purpose, mission, and goals.

Time and Experience Does Not Equal Expertise

Among the many great books and writings that have inspired me in
my exploration of intentional leadership is *Turn This Ship Around!*
by L. David Marquet,[1] a retired US Navy captain. It reminds us of
what gets in the way of developing other leaders effectively – mindset! What is a leader's current mindset about developing leadership?
Do leaders believe they can develop themselves through osmosis
or through experience only? Unfortunately, time and experience do
not equal expertise and certainly not mastery.

Technical or Leadership Skills

Another common pitfall is to spend more development investment
on technical, strategic, and technological learning and much less on
leading people and the complex dynamics of doing so. There is also
the long-held belief that development investments should be aimed
at middle managers and emerging executives and not necessarily at
senior leaders. Much more uncommon is development action for
senior leaders. Until 2000, very little deliberate, organized learning
targeted top leaders. Then, in 2008, this changed and now up to the
top 500 leaders in some organizations are provided carefully designed in-class and on-the-job leadership teachings to incorporate
into their responsibilities.

More Stretch Assignments

In many organizations, the changing paradigm related to developing other leaders has now shaped the practices to produce a well-established model to guide better outcomes. As noted earlier, this development approach generally results in a ratio of 70-20-10 per cent to guide more deliberate and tailored development activity. The 70 per cent guide places a priority on job assignments at the core of relevant, real-time "apprentice-like" learning. The challenge found in this widely used practice has been the matching of assignments and the placing of potential leaders where the stretch has been inadequate or the coaching spotty. As a result, optimal learning goals are hampered or even not achieved, making leadership pipelines weak.

Mentoring and Coaching

The 20 per cent guide calls for well-designed mentoring by the person's own leader and others. As emphasized in chapter 8, the benefits of mentoring can be staggering, especially when the matching and intentions are clearly present. People with well-chosen mentors are believed to be up to four times more successful than those who haven't chosen the best match. Mentoring has become a major component of all leader development. Many CEOs have more than one.

Classroom Learning

Meanwhile, the 10 per cent guide calls for classroom-type resources. Here, the current trend is well beyond sending someone to a course because it is popular or accessible. Business schools are now under far more scrutiny as to the relevancy of their offerings; they are responding with more effective types of content. Targeted, relevant, and current classroom programs are now emerging to meet the more intentional approach to developing other leaders to leading better and leading well.

The Big 8 capabilities evolved from multiple teaching and learning experiences as well as the inputs of many senior leaders. They have been discussed, debated, and validated across multiple sectors. In part 4, a few more explicit tools are offered that can be helpful to the reader who is pursuing self-reflection and intention to adopt one or two additional practices. These will further confirm what you are doing or perhaps encourage you to think a bit differently about what you believe. The Big 8 offer a flexible choice as to where you start. Why not start something new? Try it!

Developing Other Leaders Is Every Leader's Obligation

Requirements	Actions – Behaviors
❖ High-quality assessment of development	❖ Calibrating multiple inputs
❖ Constant and consistent feedback	❖ Mapping intentional and deliberate courses of action
❖ Mentoring mindset	❖ Inspiring others to lead, not just follow
❖ Inspiring potential in others	❖ Creating *heroes*, not being the hero

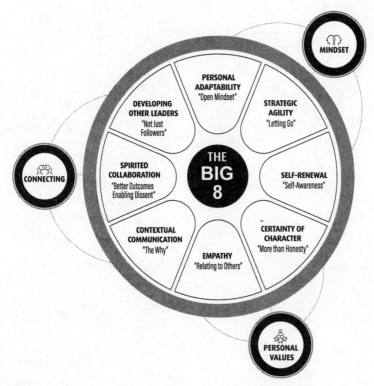

FIGURE 17. The Big 8: Mindset, Personal Values, and Connecting

PART FOUR

Leadership Starts with You – It Must Be Intentional

The measure of intelligence is the ability to change.

Albert Einstein

A Prologue to Part Four

Einstein's quote has never been more fitting. As this book asserts, we are once again in extraordinary times; our journey began with the implications arising out of the global financial crisis. That opened this book. Now, we conclude the book with another big disruption – facing the implications of the COVID-19 pandemic – and we know that other disruptions will emerge as time passes.

The theme of leadership as not being timeless emerges throughout, with numerous examples calling for leaders to self-renew as well as to lead others toward their own potential. We see many good transitions being made, as depicted by the pendulum shift in chapter 10. CEOs and leaders everywhere have been stepping up. It is impressive to witness the transformations across every sector of society. This wake-up call will continue for all.

Intentional Leadership Becomes More Critical

The time for Intentional leadership has never been more acute. Going beyond instinct to create intentions from reflection and ingenuity – this is the new norm. As we continue to discover the reshaping of our workforces and workplaces, one thing is certain among all the unpredictability: the focus on human potential as our most untapped asset will be brightly illuminated. How we inspire, motivate, and develop the potential of those we lead will challenge the way we grasp and utilize technology and how we navigate the structure of work itself. The hybrid and remote workforce will intersect and influence expectations of leaders' capabilities. Concepts of connecting well and effectively empowering others will be fundamental for all.

Digital Transformation – Everyone's Challenge

An example of digital transformation is offered by Darryl White:

> In companies like ours, we have to worry about both "inside and outside" digitalization. Inside, it's everything to drive work, make it more efficient; it's about talent, who's doing what, when, where. This is enormously important, especially in the earlier innings of the game. Outside, it's the channels and products to get to customers. What products will go to customers and how soon? Mistakes are made if you go too slow or too fast. We're still in the early phase. Meanwhile, how do we deal with digitalization while controlling the costs? It's the biggest question I get from the people we serve. How do we do all this? What are the talent models? Do we create a digital department?

Darryl is skeptical as to whether a digital department is the answer:

> We don't have a separate customer department, because all our jobs are
> about customers. If you have a technology department, it should be for
> everyone, since everyone uses and is dependent on digital technology.
> Does that mean embedding technical or digital experts in each business
> unit? Do you isolate them in a center of excellence? It's a big challenge for
> big companies: How do you organize digital? I believe the days are over of
> having the technical people over here and the business people over there.

I reminded Darryl that, less than ten years ago, the way in which
work was being organized and how leaders led talent became the
biggest barriers to adopting digital successfully. His response:

> On talent and leadership we have to ensure that candidates are capa-
> ble of doing integral enterprise work and that they embrace digital
> literacy. These two aspects are key, above all else. Candidates need
> to be foundationally strong as well as digitally adept and curious. It's
> the new basis, the new norm. We're on a journey with digitalization,
> but not there yet. It's huge. I'm on the journey personally. I've had to
> learn, ask others, go outside my comfort zone. It's not enough today
> to say you've gone paperless. The talent agenda is very important: it's
> about reskilling the people we have, not just recruiting new ones. And
> increasing digital literacy is part of it.

I am struck by how Darryl weaves in his various elements of leading,
synonymous with those revealed throughout this book. His references to the need to go beyond instinct and move to being intentional
were echoed by other leaders in our conversations. Self-renewal,
adaptability, and strategic agility were also shared by others, as were
human skills and the importance of the human dynamic.

Partnerships and Collaboration

In a different sector, for example, Meric Gertler speaks with enthusiasm about success through virtual-digital-based interaction and partnership:

> During the pandemic, our ability to carry on as a university was dependent on digitizing so much of what we do. It enabled virtual interaction at a time when personal mobility was very difficult. Many good things happened as a result: the organization kept running and fulfilled its mandate. New things happened too. Literally overnight, a whole generation of our faculty was introduced to technology-mediated teaching, learning, and partnership. Thank heaven, we had the right infrastructure for this. As our understanding of the capacity of digital tools grows, we find ourselves at the beginning of a journey toward the re-invention of undergraduate education. We've just seen an acceleration of that process over the past two years.
>
> The challenge for leadership is not to fall back on tried-and-true ways but to continue to stimulate openness and innovation in what is possible. A university is a collection of smart people who interact daily. My worry about the quality of the interaction is always foremost, so that we do not risk impairing deep understanding, mutual respect and trust, due to digital-mediated interaction and the extended absence of face-to-face interaction. The world of scholarship and research needs that reassurance. Trust is paramount in many sectors, not just the university.

What Darryl and Meric are espousing is *intentional leadership*. We find it similarly espoused by McKinsey.[1] The focus on horizontal collaboration, on strategic agility, on building teams, on letting go of the past while taking personal responsibility for self-renewal – these need fortitude to adapt and rebuild. Hearing from other leaders will be helpful in the next chapters, as we put the spotlight on the challenges in taking charge of leading in this new environment.

The Next Four Chapters

In this final part of the book, you are prompted to pause, reflect, and pose the questions for what your own intentions and renewal need to be. Within the context of your organization's purpose, what are the dynamic strategies and mission and human skills you will need to rise to the top? Leadership starts with you. If so, then it must be *intentional. Intentional leadership is hard but ever so worthwhile; and it enhances one's worthiness as a leader.*

Through the next four chapters, ideas and experiences are offered on four top imperatives and obligations for leading well. Just as Darryl and Meric offered perspectives and insights on their foremost challenges and responses, so too will others share perspectives and priorities.

FIGURE 18. The Four Top Imperatives and Obligations for Leading Well

can do better at adjusting their blind spots – as long as they trust the feedback. What gets in the way of this?

Self-awareness and leaders' renewal are a constant focus in my advisory work. Low self-awareness is such a frequent cause of leaders not excelling or even going off the rails. Yes, leaders do care about blind spots and the notion they might have a flaw in their leading. That's a fact! But where resistance exists, several factors are at play.

Having blind spots is human and natural. It's often rationalized by saying, "The issue is really someone else's and it's the other person who needs to change." Or, "It's just who they are, it's their person-ality and they cannot change." It is also common to hear: "I know I have a habit of doing this and it causes a problem. But that's just me: it's how I am, and I'll probably never change!" Of course, in this situation, leaders are reminded they are not expected to change their personalities (and couldn't change it anyway – best not to try!). However, everyone can change a behavior if they want and if the reason is worthwhile.

The ensuing discussion thus goes like this: "What you say might all be true, but in this particular organization, at this time, the be-haviors being highlighted as disruptive contradict the intention of our values, purpose, or goals. A different behavior can result in a more positive outcome and can have greater impact on people and the organization. Adjusting it is worthy and worthwhile. It results in being a better leader." Sometimes this advice works like magic because people always want to be better – even when it's hard or awkward. It is nonetheless understandable that increasing self-awareness does meet with resistance and, for some, making adjustments elicits even greater resistance at times. But trying is a gold standard.

To my knowledge, it wasn't until 1972 that self-awareness was first treated conceptually by Shelly Duval and Robert Wicklund in their book *A Theory of Objective Self Awareness*.[1] It was about focusing attention inwardly and thinking of one's impact on others. But it was also about reflecting on one's values in terms of what one stands for and cares about. Nowadays, fortunately, we hear so much more about the importance of being self-aware and how imperative it is to becoming a great leader.

Up to Four Times More Successful

From more recent research we learn that those who are self-aware are up to four times more successful than those who are not. I personally believe this, as I've observed it to be the case. Self-awareness is an observable leadership differentiator and a key to greater success. My observations also support the belief that leaders who are self-aware and know and care greatly about their impact on others tend more often to question themselves. They reflect more deliberately on their impact and whether it was positive (using reflection to understand why it was).

In the classroom or any advice-giving session, a frequent takeaway for leaders is the advice to take ten minutes to reflect on what impact you had today and ask yourself, Was it positive? It will take courage and fortitude to really be objective, especially to take certain actions or make adjustments. Courage is another gold standard. Trust is a special bonus coming from deliberately adjusted behaviors. People do notice! Leaders making adjustments quickly get past the hard part of feeling vulnerable or exposed or silly because it is offset by the positive impact that immediately becomes obvious. Just try it! Suddenly, the time taken by the reflection and intention is forgotten, such is the power of the role-modeling and humility it represents.

Many leaders I know have a wise grasp of reflection, self-awareness, and adjusting behaviors. For example, in speaking about

Self-assessment leads to learning.

how self-assessment leads to great learning, Tiff Macklem points out: "Leadership is learned. Intentional leadership begins with self-assessment. These two notions are intertwined." In other words, how is it possible to learn lessons without self-assessment and reflection? As Tiff notes: "Self-assessment can reveal hitherto unrecognized omissions or unconscious resistance to certain things just by posing to yourself some questions. Are you coachable? Do you find it hard to accept advice willingly or not take it at all? Perhaps not all the team is as positive as you, the leader, are in pursuing your vision. Maybe some are enthusiastic, while others are somewhat aloof. Why is this? Have you ever thought it might begin with you?"

Posing such questions and reflecting on them mean you are beginning to understand that leadership is learned, so Tiff says. To illustrate this point, he tells how he began his career as a research analyst, working in detail and data. Taking advice from others did not come naturally. However, in helping people solve problems, he found he was more listened to, which bolstered both confidence and career. As the boss of others, he asked himself how he would gain the support of others around him, especially now when he really needed it. The answer was to listen well and closely to others. Not inviting colleagues and staff to air their views, concerns, or give advice means "you miss the opportunity to get the value of diversity of views, which leads to a better decision in the end, with the team having confidence in the process." It is important to practice listening and being open, while welcoming feedback and demonstrating willingness to adapt, especially as the CEO. But it also means reflecting on learning moments with an openness to how it could be better. "Sometimes," he observes, "the safest place to go for increasing awareness is right in front of you – if you open your mind." It starts with you!

Feedback Is the "Breakfast of Champions"

Ron Farmer confirms the importance of feedback and self-assessment for all leaders and CEOs and their role-modeling. "CEOs and leaders can benefit enormously from feedback, but it can be tricky. Some CEOs form small groups to gain feedback – this can be very effective and even more so at times than relying on the 'all-seeing' consultant. Though consultants can develop helpful relationships." Ron has seen many CEOs who practice and show accessibility by walking around and talking to their customers and others. They positively welcome criticism, on the basis that all feedback is good. These are the same CEOs who ask the chair of the board for feedback in addition to the standard self-assessment process and don't just resist it. Getting feedback from multiple sources is part and parcel of self-awareness. It is the starting point of intentional leadership.

Jobs at the Top Are Lonely

Responding to the question about blind spots and getting senior leaders to acknowledge them or at least be aware of them, Ron's view is that "all leaders, and CEOs in particular, always say the job is lonely. Yes, one can have access to the skills of coaches and other sources of feedback, but the effectiveness depends on a relationship with one's boss – yes, including the chair of the board. [Receiving] 360-degree feedback can be helpful but not always; it too depends on trust between the leader and the mentor." Ron concludes with this important insight: "Self-awareness in leadership must be built on trust foundations with all who offer/give feedback and beyond." Trust as being central to all leaders' actions is once again confirmed.

Learn by Setbacks

Other techniques used by leaders, including CEOs, to enhance self-awareness include deliberate reflection on mistakes made or setbacks and failures experienced. Some of those we identified as defining moments at the start of this book. This is a very powerful way to increase self-awareness, but what might sometimes be lacking are the intentional and deliberate adjustments to one's behavior in other circumstances. Adjusting beliefs or mindsets that led to the mistake becomes really important. Reflecting on why a certain behavior was used, why it had a negative impact or outcome, is exercising empathy and insight. It too can be very powerful as an incentive for adjusting and as a worthy effort by a leader. Consider, for instance, the role-modeling this represents to others.

Learn from Knowing Why

A technique shared by Mary Jo Haddad weaves opportunities for gaining self-awareness into decision-making situations. "Making decisions and being intentional about how you lead is all about gaining awareness. Taking a moment to reflect on 'how things went and how they could have been better' helps build self-awareness – but the critical thing is to be intentional about adjusting for the next time. Without this reflection and adjustment, it's hard to get better." Sharing with others "the why of doing things differently also creates awareness for the team. They in turn learn to be reflective about the way they could have been better. Have the courage to put things on the table and engage the team with you as new insights are exposed."

It is understandable to think about the time and effort, the discomfort and hard work, required by reflection, self-awareness, and adjusting. Yet, as just confirmed by three CEOs and accomplished leaders, as well as by others throughout our journey, changing the way you lead so that your impact on others is positive *does result* in better outcomes. Experiencing this is magical. Those who are self-aware and who act on improving it, as we are told, are more successful than those who are not. My own experiences confirm this finding. In working with leaders, I see them generally fit into three categories:

FIGURE 19. Three Categories of Leaders

Leadership is hard – but a great privilege for those who want it!

CHAPTER TWENTY-ONE

Building Teams and Leaders: Selecting and Developing

I wish I'd moved more quickly on certain leaders. Maybe if I'd taken action sooner, the team success would have been greater.

A CEO reflecting on what they would have done differently

It used to be that, when asked what they would have done differently, CEOs would say: "I should have moved earlier on changing strategy." Now when asked, a CEO or any leader will say the same but quickly add: "I should have acted sooner on strengthening the team."

Acting more quickly does not always mean letting leaders go. But it does mean knowing and ensuring the best talent is on the team to move the agenda forward and to ensure the team's mix of skills complement the CEO's own skills. This is expected of all leaders who lead teams. In chapter 19, the concept of "turn this ship around" was introduced in the context of developing leaders, not just followers. That is the ultimate goal. There is no other role more important for a CEO, a board, or any leader than to develop other leaders.

Selecting the Best Talent

Building teams begins with selecting the best talent. Intertwined with this, however, is developing them through constant assessment to ensure they are adapting and renewing. How this is done comes in many forms of feedback – assignments, mentors, and sometimes more formal in-class customized programs such as I use in my own work. So much depends on the point-in-time, the conditions, and the context of what is expected to be delivered by the leader.

Multiple-Source Input

One of my earlier discoveries was the importance of "multisource" input. It was not too long ago that the second-level manager removed made singular decisions in choosing leaders. My early discovery experience was as chair of the governing council at the University of Toronto, where, like many universities, formal, diverse, and broadly representative search committees had significant discussion and debate of candidate qualifications from multiple perspectives. Today, the concept and practice of the multiple interviews and assessments is quite common and we do see the great value of this approach to selecting leaders and building teams.

On assessing and picking leaders, Tiff Macklem finds choosing and hiring other leaders a humbling experience. "Some candidates can draw you in and you can be blind to their gaps; others can turn you off and you just don't connect with him/her." He learned that it helped to get multiple perspectives and input from others, and this became his practice. Such other perspectives often revealed things that he'd missed altogether. He also sometimes realized that those about whom he was less enthusiastic later became successful. It's a good lesson about balancing inputs and weighing the collection of information and impressions. "Sometimes when you scratch further you find more that impresses – or less. Having other inputs can reveal this. Of course, you can often be more comfortable with inside hires for this reason. The big question in picking leaders is whether the candidate is right for the present role – because being good at the last one doesn't guarantee it. The important thing is whether the current context changed."

Has the Context Changed?

In selecting leaders, so much is at stake. Yet a common pitfall is neglecting to ask or deliberate on the questions, "What is different this time? What proven capabilities are necessary in the current context?" It's not always about the tried and true of the past. "What adaptability or renewal might be needed for now – and can the candidate truly adapt well?"

Tiff used his own experience to illustrate the importance of context and time in judging a leader's suitability. Returning to the Bank of Canada after serving as dean of the Rotman School of Management, Tiff quickly realized that a lot of water had gone under the bridge in the interim six years and that he'd have to adapt his mindset to ensure care in judging capabilities. People had changed. It was important, therefore, to open his mind about them to avoid carrying baggage from the past or relying on yesterday's assumption. He also followed the advice given to him to pause and make sure he saw the positives and negatives and how the total translated into the current requirements before judging capabilities.

A Constant Dynamic Is Change!

Building or rebuilding teams is not easy. It can reveal challenges and pitfalls encountered regularly by even the most accomplished leaders.

That is why it is so worthwhile to learn from others' insights. Being aware of changing contexts has never been more valuable than now. Changing leaders in any context can be a complex undertaking. But, as Katie Taylor points out, it doesn't need to be dreaded or resisted. Making change among leaders, she says, is an expected ongoing dynamic:

> Taking a 360-degree view of the team in the context of the whole and what is to be delivered and achieved will make one quickly realize that change is necessary. But you often realize you can't change just one thing because all the dots are connected. The context of the environment is therefore critical. Just consider how some organizations actually thrived throughout the pandemic, while others did not. It was due to their adaptability or the team's capabilities or other conditions. This becomes a central question in building or renewing teams and what to consider about the changing contexts around us. All leaders need to see that change in teams is, in some way, necessary. It's not about musical chairs but rather about the natural flow of meeting the requirements for success. Initiated change, combined with opportunities presented by reassignment and retirements, should ensure high performing teams.

Katie's wisdom underlines the reality that building teams is never static. Today's extraordinary times make this even more dynamic and harder to get right.

There Is No Grace Period Anymore

Ron Farmer strongly emphasizes the urgent pace today of building and sustaining capable teams. Through his many direct advisory involvements with CEOs, boards, and C-suite teams, Ron views strong capable teams not just as critical but also as table stakes, which he pointed out in our conversation:

Let me reinforce your point, Rose, about the obligation and responsibility for developing top leaders. There is no grace period for incoming or existing leaders, especially CEOs and senior leaders, in terms of performance, the team's strength, or succession. Today's CEOs must arrive with a plan that a board approves and that includes the right team. So, expectations are clear. Most CEOs I meet wish they'd moved faster on ensuring team capabilities were strong. The "wait and see how things turn out" approach is not credible for long. CEOs and leaders do not have this luxury. Instead, the action is to figure out what you need to complement your own strengths and then get it done. A leader cannot wait a year to form the right team. Decisions on suitable capabilities need to be made right from the start.

Building Teams Is a Leader's Biggest Challenge

These insights from Tiff, Katie, and Ron cover many critical actions and ways to think about successful leadership in building teams. While we know that many leaders place great priority on this, we also know it is hard. Few leaders ever enjoy doing all that it takes to do things well and with the desired urgency. In my own experience in picking and developing senior leaders, the biggest concern is seeing inadequate attention being paid to specific development actions, both at the start of a leader's tenure and ongoing. One of the biggest shortcomings is inattention, if not resistance, to self-assessment and self-awareness. This impedes the ability to improve the mix in a leader's team. It is vital also to pay attention to leaders' beliefs and mindsets. We are looking for leaders who believe the following:

• Leadership can be learned and leaders devote time to mentoring or being mentored;

- High performance is not an end in itself – specific capabilities do matter;
- No one leader has all the answers – ongoing learning is the "breakfast of champions";
- Being self-aware is a must for anyone to have optimal success;
- High emphasis must be placed on human skills, such as those in the Big 8, not just technical ones.

Barry Perry captures this in his views about building teams:

I'd give a different answer today to how I think about building teams than I gave ten years ago. I look for well-rounded people with strong emotional intelligence and who embrace a lot of what's happening in the world today – inclusivity, environment, climate, and so forth. Without this breadth of perspective, you cannot be a strong leader – those are table stakes now. I also watch for how people react under pressure. Leaders should know that crises, challenges, unanticipated events will happen. Boards have to trust and count on CEOs and their teams to withstand turmoil and keep the team intact through sound navigation. Stakeholders deserve it! Resilience and getting through tough times are what make real teams into heroes. It requires wisdom and staying cool with stressful decisions. It's not always that a decision made today is the only one which could have been made. Diversity of thought matters. As do positive attitudes, not being risk-adverse or adhering to the status quo, being secure in one's own abilities. People who are independent thinkers and able to contribute to decisions are what the team needs.

Getting the Assessment Right!

As you reflect on and take charge of developing your team, much will depend on getting the assessment right. That is, getting past the halo effect of past performance and digging deeper into what is needed for today. And whether the skilled leader can adapt, can build and lead teams based on their technical expertise, has a learning mindset – and, above, all, is *intentional in leading well.*

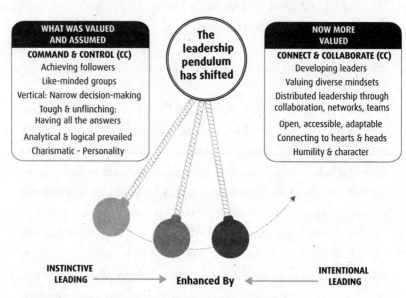

FIGURE 20. The Leadership Pendulum Has Shifted

The use of tests and 360-degree inputs are very commonplace and gaining in value, but still have pros and cons and need to be used with care and thoughtful judgments. They can augment, though never replace, the combination of techniques outlined in this chapter.

CHAPTER TWENTY-TWO

Being a Mentor and a Mentee: A Great Leader Is Both

Mentors are leaders of substance and influence who see beyond themselves to enable someone else's success. Mentees are open, teachable, and forever grateful who then "pay it forward."

The good news is that mentoring has emerged from the typical overstructured, misunderstood, and resisted ethos of learning practices. Despite breaking through, mentoring still needs constant reinforcement and encouragement.

Do You Have a Mentor?

Today, we can confirm that mentoring is moving to take up a more prominent share of typical leader development activities. This increase can be attributed to leaders' growing awareness that mentoring and different forms of giving and gaining feedback are integral to the way they lead. Other influences come from the changing workforce, where greater and different expectations for feedback continues. We reviewed in chapter 8 the outdated belief that mentoring used to be viewed as primarily for emerging leaders. This myth still exists, even though we now have so much great evidence pointing to the use of mentoring, both as a mentor and as a mentee. Chapter 8 revealed this and inspired me to share with you, the reader, the toolbox for being more intentional.

Not surprisingly, conversations with the leaders participating in this book were all rich and enlightening in different ways. They immediately and voluntarily spoke to their own use of mentoring and why they made it a priority throughout their careers. Their stories confirm the different shapes mentoring can take, as Meric Gertler describes with respect to the use of technology: "People in senior ranks often need assistance and we put students with faculty to help in such ways as optimizing the use of technologies. This accelerates the movement along the learning curve while at the same time improving the learning experience of the students." Meric also believes that a delegative and empowering form of leading lends itself more readily to a mentoring mindset. It enables the team to perform up to their full potential. This kind of mentoring is great for signaling and showing your team that you, as a leader, are committed to being the best leader you can be. It shows the work you are willing to put into their own success and growth. (Recall that in chapter 8 we referred to this as "reverse mentoring.")

Are You a Mentor?

Like many leaders, Meric embraces both senses of mentoring: being a mentor and a mentee. He provides mentoring opportunities for his team. Plus, he's also sought out opportunities as a mentee to discover more about himself and how to be a better leader: "It requires strength of character (humility) because what you are saying is, 'Boy, do I have a lot to learn.' We don't say that enough. Yet openness to being mentored is so essential to learning more about yourself, increasing self-awareness, finding better ways of leading. At the end of the day, it's about benefiting from others who, like you, have themselves been students of leadership."

As mentioned earlier, mentoring in its many forms is now widespread and widely accepted. Tiff Macklem recounts his early mentoring experiences:

> There wasn't a lot of talk about mentors back then. Often with mentors you admire certain qualities about certain people and find yourself gravitating toward them. I have had a few and still stay in touch. They know my world. A mentor is someone you really trust; someone off whom you can bounce ideas. Sometimes they simply give feedback to stiffen your spine, as if to say yes, you're on the right track. Other times they suggest you may want to consult further and reflect a bit more. The main thing is that you are not alone. And this includes board directors.

Tiff underlines how important mentoring is as you take on new and bigger assignments. "Problems are bigger, decisions are more complex, stakeholders are more demanding. You are not always prepared for this bigger level of leading and of managing."

Choose with Care

Choosing a mentor with care is a wise idea. Personal chemistry matters, of course, but credibility and trust are top of the list. A mentor's credibility comes from knowledge and wisdom as well as the experience of "having been there." Having more than one mentor can be helpful, as a leader's roles are complex, and breadth of real-time experience is needed. Katie Taylor describes what a mentor means to her:

A mentor is not a cheerleader – someone who tells you what you want to hear. Mentors need to tell you the tough stuff that can correct your course by providing feedback and discussing your thoughts on what worked or what didn't work. You should expect mentors to do their homework. Mentoring is analogous to competitive sports – taking higher performers to an even-higher level. Mentors have been instrumental in making me a better executive and now a senior leader.

Mentoring is like "paying it forward." Mentees who receive the benefits of feedback to increase self-awareness and prevent them from stumbling often want to be a mentor. Most of them do become mentors. One of the reasons I chose to mentor, as a deliberate part of what I do, is due to the many great mentors I've had all through my life and career. Witnessing the empathy, the trust, the generosity that the mentor extends is an inspiration. These are the ingredients every leader aspires to have in their desire to be worthy. Mentors are leaders of substance and influence who see beyond themselves to help others be successful.

Bringing Out the Best in People

Listen to Mary Jo Haddad reflect on her desire to mentor from early on in her career:

It starts from a mindset of bringing out the best in people. For example, knowing that a person's background is different from yours or others on a team and that you want them to have impact. Some persons often struggle in building the trusting relationship that are needed to have their perspectives accepted or even heard. My inclination is to mentor them on ways to tune in to other people. I work long and hard on those situations. As CEOs we need to take the time and energy to engage in this form of mentoring.

Mary Jo thinks of it as cultural and social integration happening in teams in real time, which expands in the workplace. The key lies in role-modeling, empathy, and helping with "the why" of what's being put forth. The benefits of this form of mentoring extend to directors of boards: "When a new director comes on to a board and has a buddy, a go-to confidant who can provide a safe place to trade or introduce ideas, test things and adapt to the new environment, then everyone wins." It's all about having a mentoring mindset.

It's Not Just the Mentor's Responsibility

Mentoring does not just happen. It has to be intentional. And it's not just the responsibility of the mentor – effective mentoring depends as well on the mentee. A mentee's expectations include a serious commitment to reflecting on their career overall. This means, in particular, reflecting on their success and impact on others as they engage in their activities and decision or struggles.

As expressed earlier in this book, just as the worthiness of a leader matters, so too does the worthiness of those being mentored. People who have a great mentor seldom forget this privilege because of what they learned. But such learning is enhanced by their own efforts. Every stage of life has so many learning opportunities. Having a great mentor is a gift, just as being a responsible mentee is about worthiness.

An Unexpected Mentoring Story Came My Way

A recent and most unexpected story of mentoring by an accomplished leader (who is both a mentor and a mentee) came my way as I was writing this chapter. It is wonderful testimony to the value of mentoring and its use by great leaders across so many sectors. I would like to tell it in full.

In May of 2019, I was invited to speak at the Leadership Academy of the Annual Meeting of the American Association for Thoracic Surgery. My topic was "Intentional Leadership and the Big 8." This was attended by faculty cardiothoracic surgeons at all levels of their careers. Dr. Joseph Dearani was in attendance to speak on "Scholarship in Innovation." He along with other speakers were present for the entire day. I was encouraged and so very impressed to witness the engagement and interest of those highly accomplished surgeons and leaders – all aspiring to being better leaders by continuous learning and renewal.

I was happily surprised when, just recently, Dr. Dearani, who is chair of the Department of Cardiovascular Surgery and past-president of the Society of Thoracic Surgeons, contacted me from the Mayo Clinic. He was seeking permission to use quotes and figures from my leadership remarks of three years ago for inclusion in a publication on surgeon mentorship that he's now authoring for a cardiothoracic surgical journal. Of course, I was delighted and honored by this interest and marveled at Dr. Dearani's leadership story and his context for quoting my concepts, especially those on mentoring. Most of all, I was attracted by Dr. Dearani's own history of being an engaged and generous mentor to numerous mentees who readily espouse his great impact on their lives and careers. Dr. Dearani is just as engaged in being a mentee, crediting many others for his own learning and success in leading.

I was very taken by Dr. Dearani's letters and stories and sought his permission to share excerpts from two of his mentoring letters that will be part of his publication.[1] Over his career, he has consistently sent letters/notes of praise or concern to colleagues, students, and residents, as well as mentors and role models, often as a follow-up to a direct conversation. This has been a core element in his leadership beliefs and practices throughout his continuing journey.

"Chasing Excellence"

Dr. Dearani's gratitude and learnings are powerfully expressed in his letters to his two mentors. He sums it up as "chasing excellence." With such examples of mentoring and its many benefits outlined in this chapter, the only remaining thought to leave with you, the reader, before moving to our final chapter, is: "If you are not a mentor or do not have a mentor, please consider getting one or being one. You will not regret it!"

CHAPTER TWENTY-THREE

So What Now?

The "so what now" is all about you trying it!
For some it will confirm what you now do.
For some it will offer another way to think and act.
For some it will inspire to let go and renew.
Trying it will be worth it!

In concluding this book about intentional leadership and the Big 8, my goal is to positively influence your leading of teams by illuminating the specific capabilities and how they are naturally applied.

Leaders who have adopted the Big 8 capabilities, even if only a few at a time, quickly discovered the leverage each provided. Examples have been given by the many leaders who have participated in classes and other groups or who have joined me in conversation. The "so what" theme arising from all the stories is about how the Big 8 enabled them to lead teams and organizations better. A common theme was about teams – it comes from the magic of getting things done successfully and with pace and positive impact. It is not the heroism of a single powerful leader or the brilliance of the CEO or any other leader within the C-suite.

As explored in the three previous chapters, the CEO or top leader needs to focus on picking and developing leaders and forming the team with the right mindset and mix of capabilities. Such leadership speaks to navigation, purpose, mission, inspiration, and mentorship. It speaks also to the CEO/leader's ability to harness, through role-modeling, courage, and fortitude, the discretionary energy of many. Finally, it speaks to the ability to *connect and collaborate* – not command and control!

> **Leading teams to success means creating heroes.**

Yes, the CEO or any senior leader has large demands and accountability. But, at the end of the day, the overall measure of great leaders is *leading the team to great success*. Technical skills, financial prowess, strategic agility, risk mitigation – these are all mandatory and constitute table stakes. However, navigating the team and creating heroes – that's the distinguishing factor and the essence of greatness in a leader.

Pause and Ponder

When I teach this program to diverse and accomplished leaders from all sectors, or in my one-on-one meetings with such leaders, this is what I ask of them: "Please pause, reflect and ponder these learnings. Pick one or two – no more than three – actions to try. It might be awkward at first, like most unfamiliar things, but your intention will overcome that, and it will pay off! Moreover, be assured! Renewing leadership capabilities or strengthening certain actions is like exercising one's muscles. They need constant honing. And being dynamic, it will decline over time if not attended to, stimulated, and exercised."

Some Top-of-Mind Examples of the Big 8 – Cited by Leaders

The last words offered in this chapter come from the accomplished leaders from whom we've heard in the previous chapters and from numerous executives who have attended many of my classes over the past decade. Their examples reflect how they identified with the Big 8 and how they exercised intentional leadership. Their stories are both inspiring and contagious, and they emphasize how and why each capability can help leaders meet today's challenges.

1. AS THE LEADER: THINK LIKE THE TEAM WHEN BUILDING THE TEAM – Start with Spirited Collaboration

For Ron Farmer, a leader should "think like a team," starting, he says, with "spirited collaboration":

> Spirited collaboration is both more important and harder these days because people are fighting for scarce resources and challenging others for them. That is why, to be a successful CEO or other leader, you must start thinking like a team would ... so do boards and their directors. You must focus on the succession process, on the candidate's capacity for horizontal leadership and for successfully leading a team – not just managing individuals!
>
> A CEO has to make different decisions when looking at teams. You've got to tweak team membership, act quickly on poor

performers, but also get rid of high performers who are getting in the way of team performance. This is critical not only to getting the job done well and with pace but also to the other team members who want to collaborate and connect well for the entire mission. In any organization there will always be those who make a team's functional performance almost impossible. Getting them off the team becomes the solution. Expect to do it early. Today's CEOs recognize that management processes need to change if you are to make teams work. And change management works best when you change management.

Ron gives us a wise reminder that the strength of the team is now what matters, not the heroism of the CEO individually nor of any one member.

2. WELCOME DISSENT AND GIVE PEOPLE SPACE – Ensure Empowerment and Differences

Mary Jo Haddad further emphasizes how the Big 8 intertwined with, and were significant to, her values. In driving her success with teams, she put diversity of opinion and allowance of dissent in debate at the core of her practices:

Some organizations have been talking about this for years, so it's not new. But doing something about it really is the test. As CEO, for example, you can recognize the diversity of a person's opinion even if they are out on a limb and way before they should continue. It might require saying "hold on, let's hear what this person has to say" – so open the dialogue! This of course requires listening and allowing discussion if it is to work. But it has a huge impactful effect on building and encouraging spirited collaboration, which is about inclusion and dissenting as part of contributing.

Marc-André Blanchard also emphasizes empowerment and giving people space:

> It's one thing to say that you're bringing in the best talent. But if they're strong people you must give them space. Otherwise, you're just creating frustration. Giving a person space means sharing. Everyone wants to make a significant contribution; make sure then that you're willing to grant space for talent to really contribute. Talent can't feel it's been put in a box. Even if they report to you, they likely have talent at least equal to yours. So along with giving space goes demonstration of trust. With talented people, when they see the CEO has trust in them, it inspires them to make the biggest contribution they can to the organization.

3. SHARE POWER AND CONTROL – Enable Distributed Leadership and Discretionary Energy

Individual heroes did exist and might have done well in some past contexts, but not in today's context. The teams become the heroes. The CEO and other leaders use aspiration, inspiration and intention to be their way of leading. Many articles and books urge us to adopt this paradigm of shifting "from single heroes to navigators and from champions to teams of heroes."[1] In a similar vein, Janice Gross Stein singles out "connecting and collaborating" through "dissent and inclusiveness" and overcoming barriers that may stand in the way: "Knowing how to lead a group through dissent may be the most important capability for leaders to master as the real value is so great when experienced. Inclusivity requires welcoming dissent. This is the meeting place of the Big 8. It goes beyond gender balance, beyond racial and social justice, even though those are centrally important. Inclusion is multidimensional and underpins the path to connecting and collaborating and the Big 8. It does take intention and fortitude."

Discretionary energy captures the "voluntary" energy that goes beyond "keeping the job" or "satisfying the boss." Leaders can buy a person's backing with pay, position, power, or fear. But a person's genius, loyalty, and tenacity are only "volunteered." Better leaders can unleash this volunteerism through distributed leadership.[2] Distributed leadership is also about inclusion and empowerment – reserving "tip of the iceberg"-type decisions for your own confirmation. This means the rest of the iceberg's great decision-making mass – 95 per cent – is made by other leaders on your team.[3]

Leaders today have to work in a more horizontal way and give control to many more people. Reluctance to give up control is one of the reasons that spirited collaboration is often impeded. By contrast, what Marc-André is saying is more than giving your team control; it's about giving them space and empowerment. We're moving past the phase in which the CEO or leader sat as a single, hierarchal hero at the top with all the power. Yet the person at the top doesn't have all the answers. The hero idea is transitioning. What's becoming visible today is that the heroes are found in the team, not in a single person. Leadership is a shared responsibility and is distributed. People brought into the organizations can therefore be the heroes who bring success. As Marc-André testifies: "We don't have enough humility at the top these days. The model of CEO as king is still with us but is transitioning. Thankfully people don't take it for granted that the CEO knows all."

4. CHECK YOUR OWN SELF-AWARENESS – Seek Feedback and Get Rid of Blind Spots

Self-awareness and blind spots are the ingredients that Mary Anne Chambers brings to the recipe for leading teams and enabling heroes. She speaks of her own awareness of a blind spot or central tendency that sometimes got in her way:

> I acknowledge a tendency to being a perfectionist and it has many aspects both good and bad in terms of leading a team. One aspect is that you can drive yourself crazy; another is that you can drive others crazy. You are your own worst enemy. In fact, you have others on your team to take the reins who would also benefit and grow from doing so. A downside of perfectionism is that people know you will step in and do it for them. But remember – it also allows them to be criticized for not getting the job done. Plus, ask yourself, who learned the most – you or them? Keeping the reins to yourself makes you exhausted at the end of the day and no one is better for it. Learning to empower and trust others in the team is very critical for any leader.

5. GO BEYOND INSTINCT AND BE INTENTIONAL – Intention Drives Purpose and Purpose Drives Intention

Darryl White frames his perspectives in the need to be intentional. Purpose, he says, is an inspiration for intention, and intention is an inspiration for purpose. A leader needs both. Intentional leaders also need sources of inspiration and proven successes along the way. For those leaders with a highly competitive nature, seeing the organization make the top of a list provides motivation and satisfaction. So too does achieving a leadership position or promoting a social issue. The competitor relishes the purpose of the energy, the run, the focus, the win! Added to this is the pride one feels in seeing teams you have encouraged achieve such successful outcomes.

Those are just a few examples of how you can chart your own
path toward intentional leadership.
You could pick one or two of the Big 8 to zero in on
OR you might just do more of the effective things you do now
OR you are prompted to think differently
OR you may even stop doing something.
The paths are many.

**IT'S YOUR OWN JOURNEY THAT NOW
CONTINUES – WITH MY BEST WISHES.**

FIGURE 21. So What Now?

Appendix

Dearani Letter #1 – "Tough Love"

This actual letter to a worried colleague (after a post-operative setback) demonstrates Dr. Dearani's empathy, wisdom, and inspiring capabilities as an impactful mentor.

> Dear Colleague,
> I could hear discouragement, despondence, and devastation in your voice on the phone this morning. I suspect the people around you at work (ICU staff), including your patients/families sense the same. Not good. This is a tough love, "pick yourself up" letter. You are settling into the game of pediatric cardiac surgery. It is a brutal game. "High rewards" coupled with "high risks." Your happiness is directly related to your sickest patient or your most disgruntled patient/family … and there is always one on the service on any given day. Unfortunately, this is the story for an entire career – it never goes away. This is one of the reasons why I emphasize the need for balance and wellness in your own life. This helps make it

all manageable. It helps you get through tough times when you are starting to question your own abilities. Your capacity to cope with unexpected outcomes or imperfect results will define your success. You must learn to rebound, and you must be able to focus and refocus when things are off the rails ... Embrace self-assessment, learn from mistakes, and move on ...

So, for the sake of all involved, be strong, be confident, and be resilient. You are smart, have wonderful hands and an unparalleled work ethic. Monitor and maintain your emotions. Being on the staff is about all this together with independent decision-making and accumulating judgement. You're on the road to a successful career. There are other patients that need our help, and we need to be there. So, stand up straight, face forward, and walk with your shoulders back. You got this. And I'll be there to support you along the way.

Joe

Dearani Letter #2

In this letter, Dr. Dearani expresses praise for a mentor from his own experience and conveys his own commitment to the influence of mentorship.

Mentorship is essential for success in almost every profession. This cannot be overemphasized in medicine, and in surgery, especially congenital heart surgery. The cardiac surgeon is challenged to meet the needs and expectations of the patient first, but also must meet the needs and expectations for education and training of the next generation. This can be a difficult balance in the current era of public reporting and transparency of outcome ...

I was very fortunate to work with two early pioneers – Drs. Gordon Danielson and Francisco Puga. Dr. Puga recently received the Mayo Distinguished Alumni award. His impact on me was profound. He had a special way of teaching and mentoring – a style that could never be found in a book. It was teaching and mentoring by example, it was tough love, it was constructive feedback, and it was endless moments of encouragement. You were inspired and just copied him … how he operated and conducted himself in the OR, how he shared technical and perioperative pearls of wisdom, and how he communicated with patients, families, colleagues … He was very demanding, with little tolerance for suboptimal performance but he was also understanding and empathetic in a way that is hard to describe … you just felt it. Dr. Puga was a professional in every sense of the word. In my congratulatory letter to him on the distinguished alumnus award I tried to acknowledge many of these discriminating qualities.

Notes

2. Game Changer #1: Increased Stakeholder Expectations

1 To explore the full 2022 Edelman Trust Barometer, see https://www.edelman.com/trust/2022-trust-barometer.

2 In the summer of 2009, a multidisciplinary group of faculty members from the Richard Ivey School of Business at the University Western Ontario began a close examination of leadership failures and successes relating to the global financial crisis. Over a nine-month period, they engaged more than 300 leaders from the business, public, and not-for-profit sectors across Canada, New York, London, and Hong Kong in open discussions on the role that organization leadership played before, during, and after the crisis. They posed one major question: "Would leadership have made a difference?" The answer they received was an unequivocal "yes." See Jeffrey Gandz, Mary Crossau, Gerard Seijts, and Carol Stephenson, *A Manifesto for Leadership Development: Leadership on Trial* (Hamilton, ON: Richard Ivey School of Business, 2010).

3 Carolyn Dewar, Scott Keller, Keven Sneader, and Kurt Strovink, "The CEO Moment – Leadership for a New Era," *McKinsey Quarterly*, 21 July 2020, https://www.mckinsey.com/featured-insights/leadership/the-ceo-moment-leadership-for-a-new-era.

3. Game Changer #2: The Ever-Changing Workforce and Workplace

1 "From Survive to Thrive: The Future of Work in a Post-Pandemic World," Deloitte Development LLC, 2021, https://www2.deloitte.com/content/dam/Deloitte/global/Documents/HumanCapital/gx-the-future-of-work-post-covid-19-poc.pdf.

2 Laurence Goasduff, "Hybrid and Remote Workers Change How They Use IT Equipment," Gartner, 13 July 2021, https://www.gartner.com/smarterwithgartner/hybrid-and-remote-workers-change-how-they-use-it-equipment.

4. Game Changer #3: Short-Lived Strategies and Digital Dominance

1 David Collis, "Why Do So Many Strategies Fail," *Harvard Business Review*, July/
August 2021, https://hbr.org/2021/07/why-do-so-many-strategies-fail.
2 "The New Digital Edge: Rethinking Strategy for the Postpandemic Era," *McKinsey
Quarterly*, 6 May 2021, https://www.mckinsey.com/business-functions/mckinsey
-digital/our-insights/the-new-digital-edge-rethinking-strategy-for-the
-postpandemic-era.

5. Dispelling Myths Takes Energy and Courage

1 My first question asked of each CEO as a mentor advisor is: "What impact have you
had in the last few months?" and not "What have you done?"
2 Carol S. Dweck, *Mindset: The New Psychology of Success* (New York: Random House,
2008).
3 We discussed the first perspective in part 1 – the external landscape of
uncontrollable and unmistakable game changers.

7. Softer Skills Do Not Improve with Just Time

1 See Richard Haythornthwaite and Ajay Banga, "The Former and Current Chairs
of Mastercard on Executing a Strategic CEO Succession," *Harvard Business Review*,
March–April 2021, https://hbr.org/2021/03/the-former-and-current-chairs-of
-mastercard-on-executing-a-strategic-ceo-succession.

8. Mentors Are Not Just for Emerging Leaders

1 This concept of reverse mentoring is a practice I have adopted over time. One
recent example was my desire to become more digital savvy and just to know more
than I did about the effective use of technological devices. My solution was to
engage a younger tech expert and have him tutor me weekly. I learned more than
I expected. He, too, received benefit in learning about my work in leadership and
leading well.

10. The Leadership Pendulum Has Shifted

1 Malcolm Gladwell, *The Tipping Point: How Little Things Can Make a Big Difference*
(New York: Little, Brown, 2002), 41.
2 Sally Horchow, "10 Life-Changing Tips from Top Connectors," *Huffpost*,
7 May 2009, last updated 17 November 2011, https://www.huffpost.com/entry
/10-life-changing-tips-fro_b_183163.

12. The Big 8 #1: Adaptability

1 Books and tools on resilience have increased many-fold over the last ten years and
are resonating with leaders everywhere. The need to master personal adaptability is
such a central driver to a leader's success. Becoming more resilient is being sought
more than ever. In the teaching classrooms where intentional leadership and the
Big 8 are offered, a key segment delving into resilience is part of the curriculum.

Significant research is evolving, showing the impact of resilience along four dimensions: mental resilience, emotional resilience, social resilience, and physical resilience.

15. The Big 8 #4: Certainty of Character

1 See note 2, chapter 2 above.
2 Ayesha Dey, "When Hiring CEOs, Focus on Character: Personal Behaviour Can Predict which Leaders Might Go Astray," *Harvard Business Review*, July/August 2022, https://hbr.org/2022/07/when-hiring-ceos-focus-on-character.

16. The Big 8 #5: Empathy

1 In the Big 8, empathy, like each of the other capabilities, pertains to each individual leader and the degree to which that person demonstrates it. While we know many organizations strive for an empathetic culture as depicted by policies and strategies – at the end of the day, the leader's *personal* leading style is tested for real-time empathy every day.

19. The Big 8 #8: Developing Other Leaders – Not Only Followers

1 L. David Marquet, *Turn This Ship Around! A True Story of Turning Followers into Leaders* (New York: Portfolio/Penguin, 2012).

Part Four: Leadership Starts with You – It Must Be Intentional

1 Carolyn Dewar, Scott Keller, Keven Sneader, and Kurt Strovink, "The CEO Moment – Leadership for a New Era," *McKinsey Quarterly*, 21 July 2020, https://www.mckinsey.com/featured-insights/leadership/the-ceo-moment -leadership-for-a-new-era. The authors ask "whether the CEOs (leaders) will continue to lead in the new ways which have recently been adopted by many. Will they seize the opportunities to renew themselves and build their teams and, in turn, their organizations in this new way?" The authors further reflect on how CEOs (leaders) have expediently and ingeniously shifted their ways, noting that the changes, which may have arisen out of necessity, nevertheless have great potential beyond the crisis.

20. Self-Reflection: Feedback, Self-Awareness, and Adjustment

1 Shelley Duval and Robert Wicklund, *A Theory of Objective Self Awareness* (New York: Academic Press, 1972).

22. Being a Mentor and a Mentee: A Great Leader Is Both

1 See the appendix for the two excerpts from Dr. Joseph Dearani's forthcoming article in the *World Journal of Pediatric and Congenital Heart Surgery* (2022, in press).

23. So What Now?

1 See Julie Battilana and Tiziana Casciaro, *Power, for All: How It Really Works and Why It's Everyone's Business* (New York: Simon & Schuster, 2021); and Frances X. Frei

and Anne Morriss, *Unleashed: The Unapologetic Leader's Guide to Empowering Everyone Around You* (Cambridge, MA: Harvard Business Review Press, 2020).

2 For more on discretionary energy, see Richard Barrett, *The Values-Driven Organization: Unleashing Human Potential for Performance and Profit* (Routledge, 2014).

3 For more on distributed leadership, see L. David Marquet, *Turn This Ship Around! A True Story of Turning Followers into Leaders* (Portfolio/Penguin, 2012).

Index

Page numbers in italics represent figures.